MW01487458

Briana

Sweet Sorrow

Embracing the Hurt
While Finding Your Joy

LEGACY POND PRESS

Sweet Sorrow © 2024 by Briana B. Hoisington. All rights reserved. No part of this book may be reproduced in any form whatsoever, by photography or xerography or by any other means, by broadcast or transmission, by translation into any kind of language, nor by recording electronically or otherwise, without permission in writing from the author, except by a reviewer, who may quote brief passages in critical articles or reviews.

Cover illustration by Mariana Foxhoven.

Scripture quotations are taken from the New American Bible, Revised Edition © 2010 by Our Sunday Visitor Publishing Division. All rights reserved.

ISBN 13: 978-1-64343-651-7
Library of Congress Catalog Number: 2024913183
Printed in the United States of America
First Printing: 2024
28 27 26 25 24   5 4 3 2 1

Legacy Pond Press
939 Seventh Street West
Saint Paul, MN 55102
(952) 829-8818

Contact Briana B. Hoisington at Facebook.com/brianahoisington for speaking engagements, book club discussions, and interviews.

Table of Contents

Introduction

"Let the word of Christ dwell in you richly, as in all wisdom you teach and admonish one another, singing psalms, hymns, and spiritual songs with gratitude in your hearts to God."

—COLOSSIANS 3:16

To live in His truth. To praise with gratitude. To dwell in hope.

Though it has several meanings, when I initially look at the word *dwell*, I sense a negative connotation. To sulk, to wallow, to sit in one space. When I look at the word *hope*, I'm filled with peace and optimism. Another chance, a brighter tomorrow, a new beginning. So, to me, these two words are opposite or contradictory. They bounce off of each other. But what if they can coexist?

My story could be someone's saving grace. My bravery and vulnerability could allow someone to speak their truth. My unwavering love for Jesus through heartache could be someone's breakthrough into discovering their own faith.

I need to share who I am and how I got here to show others that living with heartache and still finding joy is completely possible. Our minds tell us we cannot have both, but our hearts tell us they can come together to create a synchronous front.

Have my plans gone as I'd anticipated? Absolutely not. Do I wish things could have happened differently? 100 percent. Would I trade my life with anyone? Not in a thousand years.

This is my journey of sweet sorrow.

These are my people, who surround me in my day-to-day life, as well as through every trial and triumph I face.

This is me. All of me. I wrapped myself up in these pages (not with a fancy bow—more like a piece of crinkled, faded, and torn construction paper), sharing the deepest parts of my heart, hoping others will find pieces of themselves amongst my story. Amongst my ashes.

Part 1

Chapter 1

Who Am I

"For us, [the song] 'Who Am I' is a reflection of us saying to God, 'Who am I that You would love me?' . . . That's what all of us on our faith journey ask: whether we are worthy? Whether what we're bringing to the story is worth anything? The truth is that it's not. What we are learning in our lives, as we've grown older and have kids, [is] what grace looks like in our lives."

—JOSH LOVELACE,
keyboardist for Christian band NEEDTOBREATHE

I was born and raised a small-town Minnesota girl. Small town as in you know everyone, there are three bars in a two-block radius but no stoplights, and news travels fast. I am the daughter of the most amazing parents: a strong and stable dad who loves without condition, is always hands on, and taught me to take the high road and be proud of who I am; and a compassionate mom who is the epitome of a caretaker and someone I will forever admire.

I am the sister to two older brothers (plus a bonus brother "adopted" into our family who will forever be another sibling of mine). They both loved and hated me. I cried about everything and always got them in trouble, a tattletale queen. As the only girl and the baby, I was the princess. But I also loved being a tomboy. I wanted to play with my big brothers, so playing sports and being outdoors were necessities. I was, and still am, a hardcore rule-follower, totally loving structure and routine. Growing up, I was scared to try new things and always felt the need to be perfect when I did do them. My parents raised me to be confident, adventurous, and fun loving, but sometimes, I struggled not to be cautious and timid.

I loved Barbies, coloring books, and baby dolls. My best friend, Anna, and I lived at each other's houses. We had each other on speed dial and hated going more than a day without seeing each other. Her parents were like my second family. I lived in an awesome kid-filled neighborhood and was always riding my bike, building forts, playing "moonlight, starlight" (our version of nighttime hide-and-seek), and being the best of friends with everyone. It was a daily occurrence to play make-believe: a restaurant, hair salon, or school. There were no cell phones or any sorts of social media. It was just us and our imaginations. I took the simplicity for granted then. How I long to go back to those days.

High school is something I will always be glad is over. I'll admit, I had some incredible times with some incredible people. But school was hard in many ways. I did well in class and excelled in my schoolwork, always prepared for what was coming next, whether that was homework, a test to study for, or a project deadline. I have a hard time relinquishing control, so sometimes I'd take over and do the majority of a group project. To me, that meant it would be done correctly (or how I wanted it) and also completed on time. This made for lots of late nights, trips to the store for supplies, and so much stress. Looking back, I had an extreme amount of anxiety that I really didn't recognize then.

Because of this, the social game was excruciating for me. Living in a small town means that everyone knows everything, and I cannot imagine growing up with the social media culture that now exists. Friends came and went. I was terribly insecure and probably presented as arrogant and standoffish. I was always facing an internal battle, and I was losing. I wish I could have shared my true self. I wish I would have been kinder and more transparent to the world surrounding me. At this point in my life, I know I missed out on so much. I didn't always allow the good to happen.

My parents divorced the summer before my senior year. This was a huge turning point in my life. It caught my brothers and me completely off guard. From my perspective, my parents were never fighting, or even angry. I couldn't imagine not being a "family" anymore. At that point, I was the only kid still at home, so I had to share my time between houses. No matter how excruciating this change was, though, my parents always put my brothers and me first. We were their priority, and they loved us through our new normal.

As I reflect back, having my life upended at a very vulnerable age was hugely impactful. I grew up in a family of love. We always hugged our parents when we left the house, when we went to bed at night, or just because. The words *I love you* were a common occurrence, not a scarcity. We wanted to be together. We enjoyed our time with each other. Laughter was always present. The utter shock of my parents' announcement was brutal, of course, but thinking of what the future would entail was even worse.

Yet, from early on, we knew we were going to stick together through this. When vacations, holidays, marriages, in-laws, and grandkids came along, we were not going to choose between our parents. This may not be typical, but it has worked for us from the beginning. No one has been left out, and we have been able to embrace our family as one unit. Don't get me wrong, it's not always easy. There are a lot of layers to it and many perspectives to be considerate of. But I will forever be grateful to my parents for never making us choose between them. To this day, they remain lifelong friends, which is pretty beautiful to witness and, I have discovered, extremely rare.

I believe my parents' divorce fueled the fire of anxiety already living inside me. It created doubt in my intuitions, fear of the unknown, and an overwhelming feeling of being out of control. But I also believe that I was always surrounded by love. Kind words, never-ending support, encouragement, and so many beautiful memories are just a small part of what my parents gave me.

I am now a part of a blended family and have added on a stepdad. My stepdad in turn gave me a stepbrother, his wife and two kids. My three brothers gave me three sisters-in-law. They in turn blessed our family with five nephews and four nieces, and I am the aunt to three beautiful babes in heaven.

I am a wife to the most amazing man I have ever known. Luke is a man of God, full of patience, strength, and humility. He is one of nine siblings; four brothers and four sisters surround him as he holds down the middle. My in-laws grace me every day with their warm presence and welcoming spirits. I am incredibly honored to have the chance to witness a life full of faith and so much love. Luke's brothers and sisters and their spouses have filled their homes with thirty-five of our nieces and nephews, and ten sweet blessings in heaven. That is a whole lot of love we are allowed to share as their aunt and uncle.

I love lists. Bullet-pointed, neatly written, checked-off lists. I love to clean and organize, to the point that it brings me joy. I know, weird. But after suffering with anxiety for so many years, I have learned a few tricks. A cluttered environment fuels a chaotic mind. Minimize the mess and simplify spaces. This allows you not only to navigate through your house with confidence, but to take the "extra" off your mind. Outer order leads to inner calm. And lighting a candle after a hard-core cleaning session is exactly what the mind and body ordered. Like check-check, complete. And I have the candle to prove it.

I love words. I love pretty fonts and quotes. I love how just the way a sentence is put together can change your whole world. It can open your eyes to a completely new perspective. I love colors and textures. Olive green, dusty blue, rosy pink, soft gray. Even writing them, I can feel them jump off the paper. They can make me feel cozy, or at peace, or invigorated, or maybe sad. A velvet pillow, a macramé plant hanger, or a knotted rug can transform an entire room into a safe haven. And music. Oh, all the music. It can make my heart beat a little different and the stars shine a little brighter. Throwing on some Christian music and praising our Lord can do wonders for my soul.

I am a true romantic. I love a good Hallmark Christmas movie, even before the snow flies. I love hearing how couples met and their sappy love stories. My love languages are gift giving and words of affirmation (shocking, I know).

And boy oh boy, I know how to love.

I love my family. I love my friends. And I love hard.

To this day, it remains: I am a feeler. A deep, intuitive, sometimes do-not-know-my-limits feeler. A true empath. I am an anxious sort and highly sensitive. I overthink, overreact, and overworry. I take on my tribes' hearts, including their happiness and their hurt. Others' moods and reactions to situations are things I hold onto and analyze. My mind is in a constant battle with itself, searching to know if I said the right thing, shared too much, came across the wrong way, portrayed what my heart felt, hugged long enough, said "I love you" so they knew I really meant it. It is exhausting.

Who I am is who I am meant to be. So, why am I constantly digging to find confirmation? Why do I so desperately need my feelings to be validated? Why do I carry the heavy burden of justifying what I am holding inside of myself? When I follow my heart and my gut, I still doubt every move I make. Ever tear is guilt-stricken and questioned by my own mind. A lot of the time, my happiness is dependent on those surrounding me.

But truly, I shouldn't be seeking others' approval. I should be seeking God's ultimate approval, to live my life showing God working hard through me.

I will continue to love hard. To feel hard. To live with my heart on my sleeve and tears in my eyes. I am a messy mix of chaos and big love. I need to not be afraid of who I am but embrace who God made me to be.

"Come to him, a living stone, rejected by human beings but chosen and precious in the sight of God . . ."

—1 PETER 2:4

I remember writing as a young girl. I found my favorite notebook and the best pen —you know, the kind with different bright colors of ink you could choose by clicking down—and let my thoughts spill out on the page. In the beginning, I had my "diary," which consisted of all the latest gossip, my fleeting crushes, and my grievances about my annoying brothers. I would write poems and songs—and even sing them while recording on a cassette tape (boy, was I cool, and please let those tapes be at the bottom of a burn pile!).

Without even realizing it, writing became my outlet. I could share on paper so much better than I could talking to someone in person. I was able to communicate my actual feelings or opinions, and not lose my train of thought or get too anxious to speak. My pen and paper never judged me. My guard came down, and the words just flowed so effortlessly from me. I could write about anything hurting my heart or filling it up. I could let my feelings unfold before me into something that I could make sense of on paper. I wrote about my first love and my first heartbreak. Losing friends and gaining others. My parents' divorce. My move to college. My future.

I started dreaming. What did I want to be when I grew up? How could I use my writing? I always loved my English classes—especially during high school, when we were given book reports and essays as assignments. I was the nerd who couldn't wait to get home to start.

So maybe I could be an English teacher? A librarian? A book editor?

Or maybe write my own book . . . ?

That massive dream fell to the back burner as life moved on. I went to college. I chose a degree as an administrative assistant. I loved the idea of having my own desk, organized precisely with pens, pencils, paper clips, sticky notes, and color-coded planners. I thought I would be good at following directions and not having to lead. I could be in the background and not put myself out there in the spotlight.

After graduating, I got a job within months as a legal secretary at a local county attorney's office. I loved it. And I was good at it.

Then . . . life happened. I got married young, then divorced a year later. I didn't know who I was, and I needed to take the time to discover what truly made me happy.

After my divorce, I met Luke in a super-romantic storybook sort of way (note: sarcasm). Truthfully, we met at a small-town festival on the dance floor of the beer garden (an outdoor tent space where beverages were consumed). At that moment, neither of us were ready for a serious relationship, but God gave us several nudges in the right direction. Over time, our paths continued to cross, and eventually the time was right. Things moved along pretty quickly after that. Mostly because we didn't *want* to put it off any longer. We knew this was right. After a six-month engagement, we planned a February wedding in Minnesota. Like a fairy tale, it snowed a light dusting the night before the wedding and everything sparkled. The big day arrived and was absolutely perfect. Our great big love could almost be held in the hands of our guests. We were beginning our story now united as one . . . and we could not wait.

The life I had and the paths I took, along with God's plan for me, brought me to where and who I am today. My story is what led me back to my passion for sharing my thoughts and emotions on paper, hoping that they will affect someone. Maybe someone will connect to them, relate to them, and find hope from them.

So now, here we are. In the unusual yet serene quiet, I hear the seconds ticking by on the clock. The dark metal hand is consistent and steadfast as it passes by number after number. Darkness has closed in around me, and the earth stands black. Shadows keep everything hidden beneath the silver sliver of the moon and flickering streetlights.

My mind constantly spins a thousand miles an hour, but the chances to write seem few and far between. My heart feels the pull to release the weight. The timid tugs on my heart-strings are becoming a bit more determined. The need to rescue the world, I think, will actually rescue me. I collect my thoughts, and the pen hits the paper. My soul transforms itself into words that I crave to speak. Fresh, crisp lines await the black ink that flows out of the desire to heal.

I sit here on my old comfy couch, in the dimly lit living room, as the rest of the house is fast asleep. The kids' dirty clothes from the day are in piles on the floor, next to the crumbs that the dog has yet to find. There is some sort of food stain on the cushion next to me, so I scoot a little farther away. I light a candle to set a calming mood amidst the chaos. My eyes feel extremely heavy, but my heart yearns to write. The pen starts to glide.

If only I can conquer the sadness, maybe I can find the joy.

Oh, girl. The sadness cannot be conquered, but it can be shared.

And the joy will emerge.

Chapter 2

I Became a Mom

March 15, 2013

Just forty-one days after marrying my dear husband Luke, I sat in the doctor's office waiting to confirm my pregnancy. I knew I was pregnant. I could feel it in my bones. I could also tell from the amount of time I was spending getting to know my toilet. Ugh. I didn't even have Luke come along to the appointment because I was already positive I was expecting. I just hoped to get some sort of medication to stop the nausea.

I brought my mom along to hold my puke bag (and in hindsight, for moral support due to what was to come). I remember talking with my mom after the positive test results came back. She was nonchalantly skimming through a pregnancy book, when she casually said that multiples could cause this amount of sickness. We laughed it off and headed to the ultrasound room. Our doctor said we would do one, but highly doubted seeing anything because it was so early. Well, not only did we see the baby, we saw the *babies*. We were having twins!

My mom and I stopped at Walmart on the way home. We bought two onesies and two soft and cuddly stuffed giraffes.

They were the kind with a metal key that you could twist to play a lullaby. I carefully set them up on our dining room table with the ultrasound photos. Luke got home from work, and I couldn't contain myself. Our future lay before him, and he was completely unaware everything had just doubled. Everything had been set up in twos, but it wasn't registering with him. Baby A and Baby B. Two onesies. Two giraffes. Two Minnesota Twins baseball pacifiers. Luke looked at me and back at the pictures. I could almost see his mind processing the *giant* news I was sharing with him. Then, suddenly, it hit him! Shock and disbelief slowly opened up into complete happiness and bliss. Multiples did not run in our families at all. But there we were—about to be parents of two. We were over the moon. Our adventure into parenthood was just beginning, but it was happening fast. We had dreamt of our future family and were ecstatic to see that dream coming to life.

Over the next fourteen weeks, I only moved from the bed to the couch to the toilet, and occasionally to the hospital for fluids and doctor's appointments. I had *hyperemesis gravidarum*—basically severe nausea and vomiting, which in turn caused dehydration and debility. I was suffering, physically and mentally. I had to quit my job very early on in the pregnancy because I just couldn't function. We had planned on me staying home with the twins after they were born, so I was just "retiring" a little bit early.

July 2, 2013

I was twenty-two weeks and three days along. It had been a rough haul to this point, and I was up all night—just uncomfortable and uneasy—feeling mild contractions. Luke's alarm went off for work at 5:00 a.m., and we called the nurses' line at the hospital to get their thoughts. With my high-risk pregnancy, they said it would be best to just come in and get checked out. If anything, it would be for my peace of mind. We made our drive into town, even stopping at McDonald's for some delicious Cinnamelts and hash browns.

I waddled my way through the parking lot (yes, waddled at only twenty-two weeks—I looked very pregnant) to the elevator up to the second-floor women's unit. They got me hooked up to machines that would monitor both the babies and me and planned to do some blood work and possibly run some tests. A nurse came in to check on me, and I could just see her face over the top of the white hospital blanket covering my legs. But I didn't need to see her, because I heard her.

"I see the baby's hair—get the doctor. *Run!*"

I can still see the fear flash across her face. The look in her eyes as she spoke those words that will never leave my mind. Time stopped but also shattered all around us.

The babies were coming. I was ten centimeters dilated and in labor within minutes.

"Do you want us to try to save them?"

How do you ever make a decision of that magnitude, especially when you only have a split second? It is a question you cannot prepare for. But, without even speaking, my husband and I locked eyes and agreed: "Absolutely. Do everything you can."

It felt like we were being consumed in a fire of chaos. There were probably fifteen people in our small delivery room. Our local hospital was not equipped for delivering or handling such premature babies. They needed to send us to the Mayo Clinic in Rochester. The transport team was on the way. The only problem: they would land in forty-five minutes. I had to keep the babies in. The longer they were inside me, the better their chance of survival.

I didn't even think it was possible. My body was screaming at me to push. The babies were ready to come, and my body's natural response was to get them out. You never know how strong you are and what your body can do until you only have one option. I had to wait for my children. I was their mother, and I had to do everything in my power to keep them where they were safest until the team arrived.

So I did.

As quickly as the helicopter landed and the team abruptly filled our room, our handsome son, Cohen Cooper, was born at 9:20 a.m. I distinctly remember connecting eyes with our doctor after Cohen entered the world. Such an odd feeling of release. Like: *I did it. We are all okay.* But, in reality, nothing was okay. Now that her dear brother was out of her way, our daughter was very content to stay right there in my stomach. She was safe and warm and exactly where she was supposed to remain for another four months. My contractions stopped. Of course, though, for my health and hers, she had to be de-livered, so I was given Pitocin to restart my contractions. And they came back with a vengeance. Our beautiful baby girl, Cal-la Grace, arrived shortly after at 10:06 a.m. With each weigh-ing a mere one pound and four ounces, they were tiny, perfect miracles. No noise escaped our sweet babies' lips, but they were alive.

Immediately, they were whisked away. The moment you dream of, the one you have seen in the movies, where the doctor lays your newborn skin-to-skin on your chest . . . I didn't get that. I didn't get to breathe them in and feel their hearts beat against mine. Instead, their precious lives were placed into the hands of the very capable transport team. I can still see them rush from the helicopter into our room in their royal-blue uniforms, completely calm amidst the chaos. They were diligent and laser-beam focused, but still so tender with the delicate bodies that lay before them. They didn't know our tiny twins. They didn't know my husband, and they didn't know me. But they were determined to save our babies as if they were their own. I will praise them for the rest of my days for giving me the gift of time with our children. The miracle of their lives will never be lost from my heart.

Our priest was called to the hospital to give our children the beautiful sacrament of Baptism. Cohen and Calla were both in the other room with the transport team, and I saw Father Eric and my husband side by side standing over them. One of our nurses came in and asked me if I would like to see the babies being baptized. I waited for them to unlock my bed wheels and roll me next to the window. But the nurse looked at me and said, "We can only bring you there by wheelchair." Everything was very much a blur at that point, almost moving in slow motion. There was so much pain and pandemonium. And, unbeknownst to me, I was losing a lot of blood. I distinctly remember looking down at my body and seeing the babies' placentas hanging out of me. I couldn't even comprehend that they wanted me to get in a wheelchair. Again, though, a mother's heart is stronger than her body. I watched my children being welcomed into our beautiful faith and receiving the grace of the Holy Spirit.

Because the twins were delivered so very early, I needed to have surgery to remove their placentas and clean out whatever else remained that wasn't supposed to still be there. This should have been a quick fifteen-minute procedure; my husband and my mother were met by my doctor an hour and a half later. I had started hemorrhaging and lost a lot of blood. But I was stable. I remember waking up after surgery in the recovery area paralyzed with fear. It was an almost out-of-body feeling. I saw stark white curtains on either side of me. I could hear all the hustle and bustle going on around me. But it was like I couldn't speak. I was screaming inside but couldn't vocalize my agony. The next thing I knew, I woke up in my room upstairs.

I will never understand why the next events happened.

July 3, 2013

We got the call that I never even thought to anticipate. The naivety that flowed through my body made every blow an even bigger sucker punch to my gut from this point on.

Luke had gone to visit Cohen and Calla in the neonatal intensive care unit (NICU) during the day, but knowing they were in the best of hands, came back to the hospital to sit with his wife. This man. It was close to midnight, if I remember correctly, when the call came to our room on the hospital phone. Cohen had developed a massive pulmonary hemorrhage in his lungs. The doctor's words shattered our world: "Your son won't make it through the night." We moved as fast as possible to get to our baby boy.

Luke left immediately while I did all I could to get up and dress, feeling, again, out of body. I was sore, bleeding, and had just had surgery less than twenty-four hours before. Everything was swollen, and I felt like I was falling apart. My body was trying to tell me to stop, but my heart had tunnel vision. There wasn't even a doctor at the hospital at that time. Of course, I hadn't been discharged. A devastating call to my parents, followed by another frantic and desperate call asking an on-call doctor to be discharged, allowed us to leave. A wonderful nurse brought me down by wheelchair to my mom and dad awaiting me at the entrance. What should have been an hour drive turned into about a thirty-minute trip. It was the most excruciating ride of my entire life. Every thought floated through my head. It felt so surreal. I have no idea if any words were said. I just wished everything would stop and we could turn back time seventy-two hours.

July 4, 2013

I arrived in the NICU to see one of the most beautiful sights I could possibly imagine. Luke sat in the tall-backed beige recliner, so full of strength and love, holding our handsome son. Our daughter was inches away in a bright, glowing Isolette (incubator). Luke is about 6'1" and 250 pounds of muscle and man. Cohen was just tiny, weighing 249 pounds less than the rock holding him.

I gingerly sat next to my husband, trying to find some comfort for my sore body. Our baby boy was placed into my arms. His chest rose ever so slightly, and I could visibly see his heart beating in it. I couldn't even feel the weight of him in my arms, but I could *feel* him. *Cohen is my son. Our souls are connected so deeply. He is mine. And I will always be his.*

Cohen was declining quickly. His stats were dropping, but they said we could hold him as long as we liked. Then Cohen took his last breath on earth. Luke cradled him in his strong arms as he flew off on angels' wings.

In my mind, Cohen symbolizes strength and selflessness. He was determined to give his sister more space to thrive in my womb. He let her shine in the spotlight. Even being so small, he had strong hands and muscular forearms, just like Luke. He never asked for more, but without even trying, he gave us the world. (After Cohen passed, Father Eric mentioned that he'd looked up what Cohen's name meant: *priest*. Our son was destined to move mountains, whether that be here or in heaven.)

The next couple weeks were a blur. When we initially got to the hospital, we stayed in the "overnight room." It was a short hallway down maybe six doorways from our Calla girl. Hospital policy was one or two nights in the overnight room; then we would be on our own to find room and board. My heart didn't hold the capacity to think of leaving our little girl. We had just lost Cohen, and I was hanging on by a thread. I would have slept on the cold tile hallway floor before exiting the oscillating doors to the outside world. My world was six doorways down. The amazing staff at St. Mary's did all they could, and we were allowed to stay for almost two weeks. There was a bed, one dresser, a toilet, and a shower. Nonetheless, it was all we needed. Luke and I talked, prayed, and slept in restless fits. In the middle of the night, I would walk down to the dimly lit NICU, where I would watch my teeny-tiny daughter fighting for her life. Many days we weren't allowed to touch her because it was so hard on her nervous system. She was overwhelmed by too much contact, sensory overload. So I would just stare at her, taking in every piece of her beauty. A miracle lay before my eyes.

During our time in the NICU, we fully experienced every emotion you can imagine. It is difficult to describe a NICU to someone who has never stepped foot in one. You learn doctor's lingo and terminology you didn't know existed in a matter of hours. You become part of daily rounds. You watch the rhythmic dance of all the doctors and nurses, all the maintenance and cleaning staff. The beeping monitors and buzzing sounds; sterile, cold metal; and strong antiseptic smells become familiar. You know the footsteps of certain doctors coming down the halls. You begin to study the other families there beside you. You envy those who take their babies home. With just a look, you sympathize with those who come in to meet their baby for the very first time. The family room was where I first taught my husband to play cribbage. It was where I wrote all of Calla's updates on CaringBridge (an online journal where people can update their loved ones about health issues). That space held so many of my tears as I clung to my husband.

The day after Cohen passed, my body was angry with me. I was supposed to be in a hospital bed, being taken care of. I had been standing far too much and had definitely overdone it. Just three days before, I'd had life-saving surgery. I sat in a heartbroken heap on the shower seat, blood running out of my body and spinning into the drain. I was swollen and in so much pain. But I let the water wash over me, desperately hoping that God could wash away reality.

I then started to have this fairly intense pain in my breasts. I couldn't even comprehend that my milk was coming in. A woman's body is absolutely incredible. I delivered our babies eighteen weeks early, three and a half months before my due date, and my body knew what the next step was. They just ached . . . and grew. I remember asking the day nurse, "What do I do?" I began to pump. There was a tiny closet of a room for nursing mothers. The pulsing sound of the breast pump echoed through the four walls into my mind. I laid down my heart to Jesus in that room. I sent Hail Mary after Hail Mary, asking our beautiful Mother Mary to wrap me in her graces. The milk kept coming, and I couldn't keep up. I was producing enough milk for two babies. I didn't want to take the time to pump, but I knew how much it could help our girl. On daily rounds, there were talks of introducing my milk to Calla. It was such a miniscule amount; they would give 0.5 CCs every two hours, which is equivalent to about one teaspoon in a twenty-four-hour period. But it was so thrilling to feel that sense of normalcy, that progress.

The nurses, and I believe the doctors, would work twelve-hour shifts, so the transition wasn't too hard. They learned every aspect of our child's care plan, and who our child was, so we quickly became attached to them and developed relationships. We were literally putting our child's life in their hands. From this experience, I learned that God makes the most compassionate and beautiful people NICU doctors and nurses. It is a truly special calling. It was so calming to see how well they knew our child. They would recognize the tiniest difference in her growth or emotion. Calla was intubated from the moment she was born, so she couldn't cry. There was a moment late one night when I sat alone with her and her nurse. Calla seemed distraught and restless. She just couldn't get herself calm. Our nurse said, "I think she is crying." No sound could be heard, but it almost broke me right then and there. My motherly instinct wanted me to break open the Isolette and tear all the tubes and straps and monitors off and simply hold my daughter. She was pleading for her mother, and I had to stand by helpless.

Another time, Calla needed to have a PICC line (central venous catheter) placed, and as she was so tiny, the staff struggled to find a vein. Our 6'5" doctor stood over her Isolette for the procedure. Calla's poor body was poked and prodded as he desperately tried to find a vein that would hold. For three hours, our doctor was crouching and hunched over with his large hands holding that line in place. He didn't give up on her.

Some days were status quo, where Calla remained stable. It was easy to become hopeful and optimistic for the future. But we always had to be aware to guard our hearts. Other days were more challenging, and we felt we were losing her, wondering how we could make it another second.

I remember one early morning, a few of our friends had come to visit us and help Luke get our things out of the hospital and moved down the street. A room had opened up for us at the Ronald McDonald House. I chose to stay with Calla. Suddenly, alarms started buzzing and screeching down the halls. Every light was flashing, and soon organized chaos was all around me. Calla's heart rate was extremely low, and she was fading fast. The nurse kept asking me where my husband was. He wouldn't answer his phone. I couldn't get a hold of anyone. The doctors and nurses asked what measures were to be taken. Did I want them to try to revive her? Over and over: "Your husband needs to hurry." "We need to know now." I was frantic, hysterical. I finally heard the elevator doors and Luke's footsteps running down the hallway. They saved her.

The next days and weeks were filled with family and friends. The hospital policy allowed one or two people in to see Calla. At one point, a chaplain from the hospital came, and I believe there were almost twenty of us by Calla's bedside. The staff was so kind to accommodate us and our huge family. We had the biggest support group that we are forever grateful for. I look back at pictures, and you can visibly see all the love in everyone's faces as they feverishly prayed to God to save the sweet girl who lay helpless in front of them.

We had people all over the world praying for our daughter. My dear sister-in-law, Mary, was in Austria when she learned of the twins being born. My mother-in-law, Julie, was en route to meet Mary. Mary had been gone a year nannying for a family with three children. When it was time for her to come home, Julie decided to meet her in Austria and finish her trip together. This is their prayerful journey on the other side of the world through Mary's eyes:

On July 2, I got a message that Bri was in labor, followed shortly after by a phone call from my dad that the babies were born and on their way to Rochester. That was all I knew. They were alive and strong little fighters! My mom was on a plane out to see me and there was no way of contacting her until she got there. I just remember feeling so helpless and restless. I didn't know what to do. I knew my mom would want to go back home and I deeply wanted to be home too. I looked into flights, but I couldn't make any decisions until my mom arrived. When she finally did, she was exhausted from a long travel with a few delays. I didn't really know how to tell her, especially since I had such little information. By the time she arrived, it was late back home. I just told her what I knew. The babies were at one of the best hospitals in the country and Briana was okay. We both cried. It was scary being so far away with such limited communication. We couldn't really text but could mostly use email and phone calls when service was available.

Once we processed for a few minutes, we looked into changing our flights. We called the airline, but we would need to pay for an entirely new flight which was outrageously expensive. We also realized we wouldn't make it home that much earlier than our planned time of about two weeks from then.

We prayed and placed the situation in God's hands. We realized that we were planning a trip to some of the holiest destinations in the entire world. Rome, Assisi, Italy, and more. Some of the greatest saints had lived and prayed [there] and were buried there today. So many miracles take place at these holy destinations. We decided that since it wasn't possible to physically be with Luke and Briana, we would invoke the saints and angels at these holy locations to surround them with grace. Since we were in Vienna (where I had been living) for the first few days, our first trip was to St. Stephen's Cathedral. It is a gorgeous gothic cathedral with many side chapels and alters. We prayed that God's will be done . . . but please let His will be that they survive and thrive. We lit a candle.

We were still in Vienna on the fourth when we found out that Cohen had died. That was a tough day. It was particularly hard on my mom because she wasn't there for her son, Luke, in his grieving. We prayed some more and looked into flights again. My mom talked at length with my dad that day and we decided to stay (we didn't have many options) and to keep offering our prayers at these holy destinations. I did start to feel like I had a purpose. I couldn't change the situation, but I could light candles and offer all of my prayers. I know the impact that prayer can have. I've felt the warm blanket of prayers at some of my loneliest moments in life. Cohen's passing was really hard on me. I was so naïve, and I didn't even really think that them not surviving was a possibility. It felt like a punch in the gut. How could he have died? I really didn't know how to process that.

A heavy cloud was over us as we traveled. We talked frequently about trying to get home and truly felt guilty for enjoying any of the beauty around us. We made it a point to go into every Catholic church we saw and say a prayer for the twins, Luke and Briana, and everyone back home. We lit so many candles and wrote in so many "prayer intention" books. Maybe God had planned all along in His infinite plan that we were exactly where we needed to be during this hard time.

When we finally arrived home (I think the eighteenth of July), our first stop was to the hospital to see our sweet and beautiful Calla. All of the emotions filled me when I saw how truly lovely and tiny she was. My heart was bursting with love for this little being and I just wanted to protect her and help her. It was the greatest gift ever that she held on long enough for us to meet her. I also thought about Cohen and was filled with sadness that I never got to meet him earthside. It was so many emotions: guilt for not being there, deep sadness seeing how small and fragile she was, and a proud joy at the little life she was. She was strong and a fighter, that was clear.

July 21, 2013 and July 22, 2013

After nineteen days in the NICU, you kind of forget what's happening in the outside world. We were so completely focused on our sweet Calla. Day after day, we sat next to her Isolette, yearning to just hold her. But being near her gave us all we needed during those moments. Every day, even every minute, in the NICU can turn into the unexpected so quickly that you don't know what hit you. As with any "micro preemie," each day was an uphill battle. The twins were supposed to be in my belly for another four months to grow and develop. It was all such a roller coaster of challenges, triumphs, and the status quo in between.

You notice all the little things, being in that small space for so many hours. You recognize shift changes, nurses' moods, and the tension in the room. And you can feel the responsiveness and well-being of your baby, almost in your bones. Something was "off" when we got the dreaded call for a sit-down meeting with the doctor.

Luke and I grabbed each other's hands and turned down the long hallway. Everything was so sterile, even in the board room. A huge round table holding one tissue box filled most of the room. There were way more chairs than we could obviously fill, and the gaps were intimidating. I tried to make small talk as we waited for the doctor because apparently that's what I do when I get nervous. Nothing felt right. I needed to just keep breathing. But it was like the air was too thick and my lungs weren't following suit. The heavy wooden doors swung open, and our doctor sat down. She didn't want to be in that chair right then. The worst part of her job was unfolding before her.

She told us that after viewing the latest X-ray, they had realized what was causing Calla's problems. She had developed an infection in her intestines called NEC (necrotizing enterocolitis). They had warned us of this infection early on because of how serious and life threatening it can be, especially at Calla's premature gestational age. Because of this infection, she also had a perforation in her intestine, which was causing air to go into her stomach. The only way to fix the perforation was surgery. The doctor said she doubted Calla would make it through surgery, and if she did, it could cause further complications. If the surgery did go well, she still would have the NEC infection in her system; this could cause neurological development issues. Because of Calla's previously diagnosed brain bleed, this was a very significant complication.

Tears flooded from my eyes. I had all the questions in the world, but my mouth wouldn't move to ask them.

Luke and I prayed so hard for our children. We prayed for direction and guidance when huge decisions had to be made. We asked God to lead us down our path. We couldn't physically or emotionally process deciding to take Calla off of life support. The doctors would ask us day after day, and we couldn't give them an answer. We couldn't have that power over a life. But Calla gave us what we needed. She had fought so hard and showed such strength, but she was ready. She missed her big brother, and he had been patiently waiting for her. They had such a strong bond and connection from the day they were conceived, and it was too much to bear. It was too much for them to be apart. Calla just needed to give Mommy and Daddy some time.

We decided not to do the surgery. We couldn't push her any further. If she was going to die, we wanted it to happen in our arms, not on an operating table.

At about six o'clock that evening, she was placed in my arms for the first time. I was holding my beautiful baby girl. They switched her over from the oscillator to the regular ventilator so she would be easier to hold and more comfortable. I couldn't help but touch every part of her, memorize every feature, every wrinkle, every finger and toe. The nurse said that she would turn off the picture and sound on the monitors so we wouldn't be worrying at every alarm or beep. She told us that she would tell us when Calla started declining.

Luke and I switched holding her on and off for about the next seven hours. We couldn't fight off the sleep any longer, so the staff set up two reclining chairs in Calla's room to have our first and last slumber party with her. The nurse came in at about 4:30 a.m. and said her heart rate was starting to drop and become more irregular. It was almost time. We cherished every single second. Around 5:20 a.m., Calla Grace peacefully let go. Our baby girl was gone.

I felt the blood leave my body. *Please take me with you. My sweet girl, please take me with you.*

We were in the hospital with so many people but felt so very alone. All of our family came to hold Calla for their first and last time. Our very favorite nurse came in on her day off to console us and say goodbye. An organization called Now I Lay Me Down to Sleep came in and did footprints and pictures for us. We waited for the funeral home to make contact and come pick up our daughter. I held onto her until the last possible moment. I saw John, the funeral home director, round the corner down the long hallway. He looked me straight in my eyes, with so much kindness and compassion. I couldn't let go. I didn't know how. My body wouldn't move. He said, "I know it's probably no help, but I will tell you, I have twins at home. I will take care of your babies as if they are my own. They are safe with me." Somehow, God willing, I handed John my daughter, and I trusted him with her. I will be forever grateful for the comfort he gave me that day.

The babies were gone. Every reminder of them hit me in the face. My milk still pulsed inside me, waiting to feed tiny little mouths. I had a freezer full of frozen breast milk. I had a fridge packed with fresh breast milk. I know there may have been other options, but I couldn't bear it—I threw every last ounce into the garbage, along with my heart. We packed up our world and sat in silence in the car. Everyone was moving so fast around me, but I was in a slow, robotic trance.

Four days after Calla passed, we arrived at the church for the funeral. God-moments continued to fill our hearts. My dear friends' mother had passed away in 2009. Her heavenly birthday was on this very day, July 26. She was there, celebrating and welcoming the babies into heaven.

We only invited immediate family and friends to the funeral because, to be honest, I didn't know what more we could handle. I distinctly remember walking in and immediately setting my eyes on the casket. The beauty that lay before me, side by side, in gorgeous handmade gowns, was almost more than I could bear.

When we were planning the funeral and choosing the casket, I couldn't get it out of my head that my babies were going into the ground. They would be lying in the cold and damp dirt, without anyone to hold them close and keep them warm. My heart knew that their souls were already gone and in the arms of Jesus. But my heart couldn't let it go. We chose to use just one casket, lined in crisp white silk. The two giraffes that had first announced to Luke we were expecting twins, that had then joined them in the NICU inside their Isolettes, now lay next to my children in their wooden casket. I couldn't take my eyes off them. Cohen Cooper and Calla Grace, brother and sister, serenely lay in the open casket before me.

To this day, people question why we decided to do an open casket. That is a decision I would have fought for with tooth and nail to make happen. I wanted visual contact with my children for as long as possibly allowed. I wanted to memorize every detail of them.

The moment the casket closed was the worst moment of my life.

Our titles of Mom and Dad were hard to share. "How many kids do you have?" became an impossible question to answer. We felt the babies deep in our souls, held onto them with unconditional love, but had no proof on this earth that others could recognize. No proof except for scars and tears.

We were now the parents of saints.

Chapter 3

Life after Loss

Luke and I opened the front door to our home and all the evidence of our twins stared us right in the face. Beautiful baby clothes, so tiny and petite, prepared for an early arrival, filled the closet. Our bookshelves were lined with pregnancy and baby books designed to help parents new to all of this. Blankets that had been washed and ready to snuggle during midnight feedings lay next to our bed. Our family did what they could to return bassinets and baby swings and bottles. But when you have two of everything, it is inevitable that some things will remain. And now, all we held were tubs of "infant loss" books, prayer shawls, preemie clothing and diapers, and only the memories from our stay in the hospital.

I remember looking in my closet and seeing tons of recently purchased maternity clothes. My mom and I had gone shopping—it felt so good to hold some sense of normalcy with my pregnancy. I was finally upright and out of bed and ready to show off my bump. I was so proud of it and the miracles that it held. Bags of clothes with tags still on them. I looked down at my now-flat stomach, screaming at me of the reality. I lay on the closet floor sobbing, grasping at the clothes, willing this to be a nightmare I would wake up from. I gathered all my strength, used my mom as the only courage I had, and carried every last bag into the maternity store. I set the full bags of brand-new clothes on the counter, and I lost it. I told the salespeople my story and why I desperately needed to return the clothes. Their immediate kindness and concern, followed by hugs, got me through that day. I didn't know their names. They didn't know me from Adam. But they were compassionate humans who I am so grateful for.

Life crept forward. I sat sunken in my grief and this harsh reality that people kept calling my "new normal." Ew, gross. Well, my new normal consisted of life moving on for everyone around us, while it seemed to sit idly in this place of unknowns for us.

You are surrounded by people but feel completely alone. You can accomplish tasks without being mentally present. People say awful things that they don't intend to crush you with but do, this tornado of words that spirals you into depression. I know that 99 percent of the time people meant well and wanted to provide comfort in our time of sorrow. However, we heard so many terrible things come out of others' mouths, such as:

- "Well, at least you know you can get pregnant."
- "Twins would have been so hard; can you imagine?"
- "At least they weren't older."
- "You're young. You can still have more children."
- "Time heals. You'll be able to move on."
- "Are you having more kids?"
- "Everything happens for a reason."
- "It was God's will, and He has a plan."

The last one was a tough pill to swallow. Looking back, this was absolutely true and I wholeheartedly believe it. But at the time, it was just another crushing blow. *Why didn't God* choose *to save my babies? What kind of plan can it be that leaves me this broken? I need to know an answer.* I didn't even have the capacity to "just believe" at that point.

Then, something I had been absolutely dreading became reality about six weeks after Calla passed. When we found out I was having twins, we'd made the decision that I would leave my job as a legal secretary and stay home with our babies. After researching day care costs, we quickly realized that I would be working basically just to pay for day care. And we really wanted to soak in as much as we could with our children. Both of our mothers were full-time or part-time stay-at-home moms. We were very committed to this. Even knowing it would involve a lot of sacrifice, it was a path we felt drawn to and would truly bless our family. After getting so sick so fast with the pregnancy, I was not able to work. I had used as much of my sick and vacation time as was available, as well as time provided by the FMLA (Family and Medical Leave Act), to help and keep my job. But at a certain point, I quit my job early, knowing I wouldn't be going back after I delivered the twins anyway.

The sun rose the Tuesday after Labor Day, and I didn't want to open my eyes. I could not fathom having to go back to a job I hadn't anticipated returning to. I loved my work family and had received lots of love and support from them. The only problem: this wasn't part of my plan. The amount of anxiety in my body was probably very visible to the outside world. I walked into the office, right back to my same desk, my same computer, my same job. It was as if nothing had happened or changed; except *everything* had changed. I remember answering phones and transcribing documents and completing tasks mindlessly. Everyone was very kind, but I could tell they were walking on eggshells around me. I get it . . . I was a walking disaster. I think the easiest thing for them was to not bring it up, and to move forward in the work environment as if I weren't on the brink of a mental breakdown. I can genuinely say that I don't blame anyone. This was unknown territory for me as well.

When I sat down in my car at the end of the workday, I would take a deep breath and the tears would stream down my face. I wanted to talk about my babies. I wanted to hear their names. I wanted to scream to the heavens that I was not okay. But I also understood that a job needed to be done. My employers were so generous to allow me to return to my job after being gone for so many months. Everyone in that office had gone through heartache and suffering. I was not the only one. And everyone handles grief and tragedy so differently. There isn't a step-by-step manual on how life should be lived, especially during times of loss. Looking back, my time back at work was excruciating. I felt invisible at times. But to no one's fault.

Grief and trauma can make or break a marriage. I have seen firsthand how infertility, loss, and death can tear couples apart.

Luke and I had just gotten married. I delivered our twins on our five-month wedding anniversary. There was no honeymoon period. We barely knew what it was like to live together. Every moment since our wedding had been consumed by pregnancy sickness, hospital visits, bed rest, and the arrival of our twins. We hadn't had the time and opportunity to soak in married life. We were now at a crossroads where we had to figure out what was next. We had to face our new reality: being home with empty arms.

I remember a moment in the NICU. We had just lost Cohen, and Calla was fighting for her life. We were living for her. We spent eighteen hours a day in the NICU by her bedside, only going to the Ronald McDonald House to shower and sleep. Even in our current state of shock, denial, and enough adrenaline running through us to keep going, we were grieving differently. I wanted to talk through every detail. I needed to explain every feeling and every thought. Luke was quite the opposite. He listened, observed, and took it all in. When he spoke, it was usually pretty powerful and full of wisdom. But I couldn't wait for him to process everything. I was dying inside.

After losing the twins, we took on each new day with an opposite approach. I am an external healer, and he is internal. But for better or for worse, we were committed to each other and our marriage. We were determined to push through together and lean in, rather than pull away. God helped us meet in the middle. God became our priority. We turned over the reins and held onto each other. Luke never stopped loving me. When I was at my lowest, barely hanging on, and probably not the best wife, he didn't leave. Instead of walking out, he chose to open the door. He sat with me.

We grieved differently, but we grieved together.

"I wanna hold you close but never hold you back . . . just like the banks to the river."

—NEEDTOBREATHE, "BANKS"

Chapter 4

Abide

Growing up, I didn't live in my faith. I believed, but almost in secret. I went through the motions and attended church on major holidays with my family. I vaguely remember the incredibly fast pace that our priest used when speaking, how I felt when my brothers were told not to cross the invisible line my dad had placed on the pew, and the number of steps it took to walk to the front of the church for Communion. I learned about Adam and Eve, Noah's ark, Jesus and His birth, and more "famous" biblical events. I memorized prayers I needed to and knelt, stood, and sat when I was supposed to during Mass. But I wasn't learning, growing, or stepping into my faith in the slightest. I lived a life about me and my surroundings, and God was never in the forefront of my mind. I didn't bother to learn more about Him, and He definitely wasn't my priority.

My childhood was really good. I have the best memories with my family and friends. The losses I endured were "expected," elderly grandparents and great-grandparents. There was no abuse or major trauma. I always felt safe, wanted, and loved. I chose my path, and through free will, God let me take it. I lived my life believing in God, but my life was going along just fine on my own. I *thought* I didn't need Him. There were no huge life-changing moments I suffered or experienced that made me search for more.

Little did I know. Seriously.

My story unfolded before me. Even after I turned my back on Him, ignoring His words and plans for me, God gave me Luke. Through my incredible husband, I was given the opportunity to search my soul for my faith. I was so intrigued by Luke's complete devotion to God. Luke is patient and kind, always willing to teach me more about the immense depth of our beliefs. I started growing spiritually and was yearning for that. But I still felt very cautious, even almost afraid.

My story continued, and it is mighty powerful.

God gave me my purpose.

He made me a mother.

And then He took it away.

I was down on my knees, begging. I was desperate for healing. For forgiveness. I pleaded with Him for answers and understanding. I was hopelessly drowning. I was fighting a losing battle. For days, and then weeks, I sat in my sorrow. I lived and breathed my hurt. It was going to kill me.

In that moment, I had a choice to make. Either way, I was going to carry the suffering with me. But I had to choose if I'd hold on to that deceptive feeling of control and do it on my own. Or, would I surrender?

And that was the moment. The moment I'd pushed away all those years. The moment my soul was craving . . .

I allowed myself to be God's child.

I always had been His, but I finally opened my heart and fully turned to Him. I was no longer living in my independence. I couldn't be selfish anymore. I was now a mother, whether my children were here on earth with me or in the arms of Jesus in heaven. I allowed my brokenness to be held in His hands. God became my refuge. I developed a personal, intimate relationship with Him. It took me so many years to realize that trying to do it all on my own was a false reality, and the walls I'd put up to protect myself were crumbling. I seemed to be running in the opposite direction of God, but truthfully, I was running right toward Him. My walls came down, and I now let God guard my heart and place His armor over me.

Don't get me wrong. I still felt immeasurable pain and sadness. There was still darkness. But I learned there is always light. It may be small and dim, but it conquers the darkness. I try to shine God's light through the way I love and live. I follow the desires of Jesus Christ and I count my blessings. No matter how hard my day is, or how exhausted and defeated I may feel, I try to find something to be grateful for.

Life is scary. And so darn hard. People leave this world too soon. People get sick. Hate is too common. Bad things just happen. And we are all human, so we make mistakes. Original sin caused the fall, which gave us a broken world. It separated us from God and made us sinners. But knowing His truth and that our beautiful salvation lies within Him brings me hope to keep fighting.

We need to drop to our knees when it's too hard to stand, because we have faith. We need to fight our hardest battles, because we have hope. And we need to give kindness and serve others, because we have love.

I don't always understand why things happen. I don't always agree with them. But I know my God, and I know He is good. So, I trust Him.

Faith is our strength and belief in our Lord. Hope keeps us moving forward. And love is what binds us to heaven while we live on this earth.

Love each other and love yourself and let the beauty of this spread in the wind.

"So faith, hope, love remain, these three; but the greatest of these is love . . ."

—1 CORINTHIANS 13:13

My brokenness brought me to You, God. The hurt showed me Your grace. The pain gave me Your heart. My worst days brought me to find joy and peace within You. Your arms didn't let me fall when I had no strength left to stand. You brought me to kneel before You.

Jesus, You have never left me. Even when I was lost. When we weren't having conversations the way we should be. When I thought I could do it on my own. When I lost all hope. When I was hanging on by a thread.

You never stopped fighting for me. When I finally slowed down and took a moment to just listen, I heard Your voice. You know when my heart is too heavy; too heavy to pull my way through to the next step. You take my hand and we do it together.

My grief led me back to You. I always have my constant in You. Thank you for never letting go.

Chapter 5

Godspeed ...
Sweet Dreams

From the mouth of my courageous husband, Luke:

My wife carried our babies. Through grit and determination, she pushed through a difficult pregnancy as they grew inside of her. She went through the most intense labor and premature delivery. I felt like I almost couldn't compare my grief to hers. Briana felt our children move inside her and their hearts beat along next to hers. I am their dad. I love them with everything I have. But you never hear how a father grieves.

How can I protect my family?

How can I support and care for the woman I love so deeply when I'm dying inside?

How can I communicate with my wife when I feel so distant and closed off?

How do I go back to work?

How do I face people?

How do I move forward?

All I wanted to do was forget. Not my children, because that's not humanly possible. But I wanted to forget the intense pain that I felt from losing them. I tried to shove it down into the deepest part of me so that I wouldn't have to feel. I didn't want to talk about it, but that was killing my wife. I lived in a constant state of fear and worry for her. But losing my little babies damaged me. It made me hard, and I lost my compassion for others. I was numb. My instinct, whether right or wrong, was to run away.

Three weeks after losing Cohen and Calla, I returned to work. I knew I had to, but it was unimaginably hard. I was broken, and I knew everyone would see right through the mask I wore that said, "I'm fine." I held my breath as I walked into the job trailer, anticipating every question about to be thrown at me. Instead, I was met with more of a feeling of discomfort and everyone not knowing what to say. Understandably so. Every coworker wanted to be there to support and care for us. I just couldn't talk about it. I knew the pain that would follow every conversation. I couldn't say the words out loud. Maybe then it wouldn't be real.

Luke's coworker and dear friend, Travis, shared this:

As a parent myself, I cannot imagine the loss Luke and Bri were going through. Witnessing their pain was heartbreaking. We all had a feeling of helplessness. Seeing Luke at work after the loss of the twins offered us a small glimpse into his struggle to maintain some semblance of normalcy amid his profound grief. Luke didn't talk much about the twins, but I think he internalized it as a way to be Bri's support system. He was so worried about her. Watching him carry on with his job duties might have underscored the resilience and inner strength it took to cope with such a tragic loss. I know that Luke's deep faith and love for his family are what pushed him through those earliest days of grief. Those same things will continue to be the strong foundation their family leans on.

Luke:

I needed to put my feelings aside to take care of my wife. She was home suffering in bed and I couldn't be there for her. I wanted to take away all of the pain and heartache. I wanted to wrap her in my arms and protect her from the reality we were living. But I couldn't because I was consumed by my own heartache. So instead, I put up every wall, put my head down, and went to work. I did the only thing I knew how to in that moment. Honestly, I didn't have anything left in me. The least I could do was provide financially for my family. I could keep a roof over our heads and food in our bellies.

How am I going to lead my family through this?

And the answer I finally came to is this: I am not. At least not alone. I am going to lead them through God.

God created man in His own image. He created man with a purpose.

God made me to be strong (1 Corinthians 16:13) and courageous (Joshua 1:9), compassionate (1 Peter 3:7, Psalms 103:13) and honorable (Proverbs 20:7, Philippians 4:8). He made me to serve sacrificially (Ephesians 5:25) and to provide (1 Timothy 5:8).

I was created to love (Matthew 22:37–39).

In Genesis 2:24, I am to be a husband.

In Proverbs 23:24, Ephesians 6:4, and Hebrews 12:7, I am to be a father.

I chose to love my wife even more. I listened and comforted her. Even when it was impossibly hard for me to talk through things, I tried. I tried because she deserved my effort. We leaned on each other and turned toward God. It is still hard, and it always will be. But we choose to let our loss pull us together instead of pull us apart. I talk and pray to my babies often.

I love Briana more and more every single day. She has shown me how powerful it is to share our story and our hearts. She isn't afraid to say their names and be open and vulnerable. I have a lot to learn from her. She loves, and she loves hard. I cannot wait to witness the reunion between her and our twins. I can almost see them running toward her as she squats down and pulls them into her arms.

I have learned that although we have suffered great loss, we also have experienced great love. I miss them every minute of the day. But I know I will see them again.

Chapter 6

Our Rainbow

Our dreams of holding our babies in our arms and watching them grow didn't fade away. We yearned to have more children. But the road wasn't going to be easy.

Words like *infertility* and *incompetent cervix* spewed out of doctors' mouths, and I wished they would just float away with the wind. I developed Asherman's syndrome after having the twins in such an unexpected, traumatic, and rapid delivery. It's a condition where scar tissue builds up in the uterus, almost causing walls to form. It essentially made rooms in my uterus, and the space to fit a baby would be too small. A surgeon would need to open it up. It would be incredibly dangerous if my placenta implanted into one of those walls of scar tissue.

I am a fixer. When there is a problem, I want to find the solution. I am a very impatient person, and waiting is not my forte. So, we found the problem, and now we could fix it.

Surgery after surgery followed, trying to prepare my body to carry a child again. The follow-up appointment after each surgery presented the same result: unsuccessful. I was starting to lose my strength to face this battle. But Luke and I weren't giving up. The fifth surgery came, and with every wall up to guard my heart, we finally heard them say the surgery was a success. It wasn't 100 percent perfect, but they felt confident enough to give us the go-ahead to try to conceive.

March 11, 2014

Within two months of the wonderful news of my successful surgery, and just four days shy of the anniversary of finding out we were pregnant with the twins, I held a positive pregnancy test in my hands. It didn't take long to realize that this pregnancy would be like my last pregnancy. Apparently, there is no sense in me trying to have a "normal" or predictable pregnancy—my body made sure to be uncontrollably ill for the first eighteen weeks. Once again, I quit my job. Déjà vu.

At twenty weeks' gestation, my darn "incompetent cervix" reared its ugly head and a cerclage was placed—basically, my cervix was stitched closed to hold the baby in—followed shortly after by modified bed rest. It wasn't required, but we thought we should do anything we could to keep our baby girl safe and sound. We set up a mattress in our living room for me to try to get through the months to come. I watched a *lot* of TV, played too many games of Farkle with my family, registered for our baby shower, and tried not to go absolutely bonkers. My dear puppy, Reecy, was such a saving grace for me through all our ups and downs. She is a Morkie (Maltese/Yorkie mix), only about ten pounds, and such a little lover. She was my companion and never left my side. She rather enjoyed having a queen-size bed in the living room.

Around twenty-four weeks along, I developed gestational diabetes. And lucky me, not just the kind controlled by diet. Instead, I tested my blood sugar six to eight times and did three shots of insulin a day. I remember being pretty livid when we found this out. *Are you kidding me? Diabetes. Can I not catch a break? I just want to eat the darn cupcake!* Luke took me out to breakfast at Perkins after our appointment and I bawled in the booth. I was angry, but I was also just sad. I was finally feeling human again after being so sick, and it was one more thing. It seems so petty now. And obviously all so worth it, because I would do anything to bring our sweet girl home. But at the time, I wanted to scream. I wanted to have the tiniest sliver of a normal pregnancy.

Going through another intense and grueling pregnancy easily allowed my mind to ask why God was punishing me. *Was I not meant to be a mom to earthside children? Are all of my past mistakes and faults creeping into my future plans? When will it end?* I doubted God's love for me, and I was so angry with Him. I started regretting being pregnant and wishing it away. It breaks me, utterly breaks me, to write those words. How could I ever be so ungrateful and selfish to deny the miracle of life that God placed inside me? After so much heartbreak, how could I feel so unattached to my current situation? The guilt that plagued me was unbearable.

Then there was the anxiety. It flowed so heavily through my veins; it was almost palpable. After losing children, you are constantly fearing another goodbye. Every movement or lack thereof made me start to worry. I had weekly appointments, all including ultrasounds, to help calm my nerves. I will forever be grateful to my doctors and nurses for their unwavering patience and compassion. They took care of my body and my baby's body inside of me, by providing medical guidance and services. But they also took care of my heart. They listened to me and heard my concerns. They allowed me to feel my feelings, completely justifying them, while filling my heart with comfort and peace.

Dr. Howell wrote:

When I first met Briana, I knew her history. I knew her losses. She was very anxious, rightfully so, and desperately wanted to grow her family. We made a plan and started taking the necessary steps.

Briana always seemed to be on the 10 percent chance side of medical history. It wasn't just the initial loss of her twins, but all the losses and complications that followed. None of the results were as good as we had hoped, and frankly, would have usually expected. It was so frustrating that we couldn't get her Asherman's to resolve, which would have allowed her to have more children.

You cannot understand joy without the existence of pain. I thoroughly believe this. Without obstacles, problems, and trials, you don't fully appreciate the joys of life. Briana's story expresses this.

God had big plans for us. All of my suffering was used for the light that was shining through the darkness. The cracks in my brokenness allowed the small glimpses of God's goodness to sneak through. He never left me. No matter how hard I pushed away and denied His love, He remained.

"Give Him your mountain and hold on when God tells it to move."

—ADDIE LEHRKE,
my soul sister, who is filled with beauty and light

October 31, 2014

The day had arrived. Finally. A C-section was scheduled for Halloween, but my baby girl was coming either way, as my water broke the very same morning. My nervous heart found it as God confirming that day was the day. Contractions started in the middle of the night. I got up to go to the bathroom for the tenth time, and there was a lot of fluid running down my leg. I remember calling to Luke from the bathroom, "I think I just peed my pants." I heard giggles from the other room. But we quickly realized it was much more than that. We went into the hospital about an hour earlier than our scheduled time to arrive for my C-section.

My doctor said he wasn't surprised that I would make this interesting. I remember getting into the operating room and feeling a sense of panic rush through my body. Memories flashed through my mind. My heart was racing and my breath became quick and stressed. The oxygen mask covered my mouth as tears ran into my hair. Lisa, one of the dear nurses who'd taken care of me with Cohen and Calla, stood beside me at my request. Her warm smile and gentle presence soothed my nerves. She held my hand and rubbed my thumb as we took slow, deep breaths together. I will never be able to thank her for what she gave me in that moment. She allowed me to feel the strength in my body and the love that surrounded us. She almost gave me permission to hope and embrace the miracle about to happen.

Since the cerclage had been placed at twenty weeks, prior to the C-section, the doctor needed to remove the stitches. Luke was asked to leave the room for this short procedure, but he would be called right back in. Well, because my uterus was contracting after officially going into labor, my cervix was twisted, which wrapped and tangled the stitches. The removal took almost forty-five minutes. When it was finally over, my incredible doctor grabbed my hand, squeezed it hard, and looked at me with a smile on his face. He said, "Are you ready to do this? Let's get this baby girl out."

My strong and courageous husband, dressed head to toe in blue scrubs, stood beside me, kissing my forehead, wiping my tears, and holding my hand. No words escaped his lips, but the conversation we held between our eyes was powerful. Every moment we had endured, all the heartache and loss, along with all the joy and love, sparked between us. It was time.

Penelope Lacen made her entrance into this world. The cries that filled the operating room I think only angels could sing. She was a little peanut at five pounds and nine ounces, but full of sass and strength. Penelope Lacen fit her perfectly, with her middle name made up of letters from her big brother's and sister's names. She was a golden ray of sunshine in a heavy world. She carried so much love and so much light. She was absolutely perfect. A rainbow baby is one born following the loss of a child. In the real world, a beautiful and bright rainbow follows a storm and gives hope of things getting better . . . A rainbow baby brings light but by no means replaces the baby in heaven. Penelope was my rainbow baby.

At nine years old, Penelope is still the brightest light in the room. She is intuitive, compassionate, nurturing, and kind. She is a true beauty. She is a lover of all animals and all people. She lives with her eyes wide open, full of innocence and adventure. And one of my favorite things: her faith runs so purely out of her. Penelope is so deeply connected to her big brother and sister. She talks about Cohen and Calla as the part of our family that they are, as if they're here with her. They share such a bond, and I believe she feels their presence, guidance, and love every single day. Heaven isn't so far away in her eyes, and it's breathtaking.

Chapter 7

His Timing, Not Mine

Penelope needed a sibling. *Here we go again.*

My "syndrome" gathered strength for Round 2. Too many surgeries to count filled my medical chart. I was trying to weave together motherhood, grief, and this desire to grow our family. I was overwhelmed and exhausted.

February 4, 2016

I sat on the cold leather chair in the sterile white office with doctors who knew my entire story. They knew me, my husband, my daughter. They knew the twins. They knew my life. They were attached. Tears rolled down their faces. The scar tissue was back, and there was even more of it. No more surgeries could be done. There wasn't anything else they could try. Chances of getting pregnant on our own were extremely decreased because of the syndrome. But even worse, the risks and complications had increased. It could be life threatening not only to our child, but to me. Pregnancy was not advised.

Now what? It was hard to breathe as they handed me pamphlets for adoption. My head was spinning and my heart was breaking. We longed to have another sibling for Penelope. To not be able to carry a child and feel their sweet body moving so gracefully inside of me—a bond that is like no other—I couldn't have that again. Knowing now that my pregnancy with Penelope had been my last, I felt this incredible guilt rush over me. I hadn't embraced what my body had been doing for me. I'd complained and prayed it would stop. All the while, a miracle grew, because God knew I needed her.

And God knew we needed our baby boy.

We had spoken with a family I knew in a town nearby who had adopted several children of their own. We had no clue where to begin. Through their recommendation, we made an appointment with a Christian-based adoption agency.

At the first meeting, we felt a deep sense of care and purpose within the organization. We loved what they stood for and how personal it felt. A ream of paper was handed to us, which was just the beginning of the mounds of paperwork we would eventually complete.

The process began. We completed rigorous face-to-face interviews, along with lengthy essays and pages of questionnaires. The caseworker came to evaluate our homelife and the environment a baby would be coming into. We then made our adoption book—basically all your life in pictures and words, "selling" your family to birth parents on why they should choose you. This book is the first thing they see when deciding on a home for their child. Talk about pressure.

Shortly after announcing our adoption goals to the social media world, we were contacted by a family member. A woman close to her was expecting and planning to place her baby for adoption. She saw our story on Facebook and was super interested in meeting us. We were so thrilled and couldn't believe how quickly things progressed. And to top it off, she was having twins. Everything moved forward, and the girls were due in October 2016. I went along to her doctor's appointments, and we were in contact often. But right before her due date, she called to tell us she had changed her mind and was going to keep her babies. Our hearts dropped in our chests. Obviously, my mama heart knew how hard it was to say goodbye. I understood her excruciating decision. I respected her for choosing life and for choosing her role as a mother. But it was heartbreaking. We had already purchased things for them. We had named them. We had big plans and dreams for them, and again, they never came home.

I was ready to throw in the towel. I quit. I couldn't do this anymore. I didn't want to pursue adoption. Penelope was such a blessing to us, and I was so grateful for her. We would be so happy with our little family.

But God wasn't done with us. He tugged on my heart and His voice echoed through my mind. *Don't give up yet.*

We stayed the course. I made a second adoption book, because our first one had become dated over the year as it was paged through by moms who'd chosen different families. And then, we continued to wait.

December 22, 2017

After almost two years of waiting on the adoption list, and three days before Christmas, we got the call from our caseworker. I was home with Penelope, while Luke was at work. The caseworker said a birth mom had chosen our family and she was due in two weeks. I am not actually sure if I said comprehensible words then. I am pretty positive it was a mixture of crying and screaming.

After a frantic, hysterical call to my husband, and a call back to our caseworker in a more level-headed state, we found out the birth mom wanted to meet with us. Two days later, we sat at a Perkins completely unaware of what the heck we were doing. It was surreal. But we told her our story. We told her who we were and why we were sitting at that table across from her. We shared our hearts.

December 29, 2017

We sat in the hospital waiting room at the edge of our seats. A C-section was scheduled, and our son was in the next room being delivered. My legs were bouncing, as if I were pacing sitting down.

After what seemed like days, Maclen Marion was born. At seven pounds, thirteen ounces, he came out with a full head of hair and was the most handsome thing you have ever seen.

We knew Maclen's middle name would be Marion, after his dad's and great-great-grandpa's middle name, so an *M* first name seemed fitting. We finally chose his name, as with all three of our other children, by looking through a book. It jumped off the page. We wanted to spell it as simply as possible yet keep the boldness of it. After announcing his birth, a friend reached out and said, "I think it's beautiful how Lacen is in Maclen's name." My jaw hit the floor. God arranged the "choosing" of our son's name. And to think, I still sometimes believe we are in control of our plans. Ha.

I will always remember the moment I laid eyes on our son. I walked into that hospital room, and the hearts of two mothers intertwined over the miracle of life that connected them. I squeezed her hand and we locked eyes. Without words ever passing through our lips, a silent understanding settled between us.

Luke and I were brought to our own hospital room, where Maclen was given his first bath. He cooed and we melted under the soothing warm water. We held him and loved on him for hours, as we shared the news with our families. We couldn't wait to bring him home. Until plans changed.

Things started to get confusing. Our birth mom's boyfriend wasn't there for Maclen's birth and hadn't shown up until hours later. Suddenly, our caseworker came in and I didn't like the look on her face. My stomach felt sick. Our birth mom's boyfriend and his mother convinced her that we were trying to trick them into taking their baby. They wanted a paternity test to determine if Maclen was biologically his. They were taking Maclen home.

Home. What do you mean home? Our home is his home.

I remember walking out of the hospital and going down in the elevator. I couldn't speak. I was hysterically sobbing, thinking *I cannot leave a hospital like this again . . . empty-handed.* I thought we would never see him again.

January 9, 2018

We weren't able to initiate the paternity test. The whole process was completely out of our control. The waiting game was excruciating. After a devastating ten days since we'd left the hospital without our son, our caseworker's name showed up on my caller ID. My hands were shaking, and I could barely accept the call. But I did, and I heard her words loud and clear, almost in slow motion. The paternity test showed our birth mom's boyfriend was not the father. Our birth mom said we could pick up Maclen in the morning.

I am fairly certain neither of us slept. I willed the sun to finally rise so we could make the trip. We reluctantly stopped and bought a pack of diapers and some baby formula at Target, still trying to protect ourselves from loss. We walked into a quaint little church on that chilly Saturday morning. It was completely quiet and completely peaceful. We walked down the dark hallway, casually saying hello to the pastor along the way, as if we weren't about to embark on a huge, life-changing journey and today was just another day. We saw our caseworker round the corner with a car seat in her arm. Our baby boy was dressed in a too-big bright-red fuzzy sleeper. I was bursting inside. It felt so surreal. "Do we really just get to take him home? It's like we are stealing him or something." I couldn't wait to unstrap him and scoop him into my arms. He was so beautiful. We opened up the sleeper to change his diaper, and underneath, to our astonishment, he wore a simple white onesie that read, "I love my mom and dad."

Everything in the world felt right.

Our Mac came home to us through the selfless love of a mom who trusted us with her most prized possession. She didn't give him away. She chose her baby's heart over her own. She made the decision to let our family become a part of hers. We will forever be grateful and honored that she chose us.

At six years old, Maclen is all boy. He loves trucks, dirt, superheroes, and football. He loves being rough and tough. He is incredibly smart and full of witty comments. Being ridiculously stubborn and persistent, he can make me laugh and cry in the same day. But he is so full of the fiercest kind of love.

He can be as sweet as honey, when he isn't stinging like a bee. His curly hair is irresistible, and his smile will melt you. (Especially with the gap between his front teeth, one chipped from when he ran just a bit too fast and the door broke his fall.) He is inquisitive, adventurous, charming, and built like a Mack truck (which makes his name very fitting).

Over the years, so many people have commented on our family. How much Maclen looks like and is built like his dad. For those who have never met Luke, know that he is a giant of a man. He provides that level of protection you didn't know you craved just by being in his presence. He has huge hands that never cease to amaze and surprise others. He is a solid man of muscle and strength. And Mac is growing up to be a perfect match to his daddy. Over three years younger than his sister, he is already almost as tall as her, and recently passed her in weight. We have to buy shorts and pants a few sizes bigger just to get over that cute butt of his; much like his dad. Then people comment on the color of my skin, in the most respectful and kind manner, saying it almost matches his bronzed caramel skin, especially in my extra-tan summer months. God knew our family would one day be together and our puzzle pieces all match.

"I, then, a prisoner for the Lord, urge you to live in a manner worthy of the call you have received, with all humility and gentleness, with patience, bearing with one another through love, striving to preserve the unity of the spirit through the bond of peace."

—EPHESIANS 4:1–3

Cohen Cooper.

Calla Grace.

Penelope Lacen.

Maclen Marion.

All brought into our family differently.

Natural delivery. C-section. Adoption.

All equally loved, fiercely and unconditionally.

As Penelope started kindergarten, my heart ached knowing Cohen and Calla never took that first nervous step into school. As Maclen learned to ride his bike, tears fell knowing I never kissed Cohen and Calla's scraped knees.

Big, monumental, beautiful days . . . normal, routine, perfect moments . . . and everything in between . . . all lost in grief.

For the moments that don't seem like anything but are everything.

My arms will always feel a weight missing.

My house will always feel a little empty.

My soul will always search for something it lost.

But my heart has never been fuller.

Through faith and trust and enormous amounts of grace, I'm learning to let go of the control my mind wishes to possess. Seeking God in every endeavor that comes before me without hesitation or desire to do it on my own will lead me toward Him.

We grew to a family of six, and God orchestrated every single note. Nothing random or coincidental. He knew my story before I was born.

He knew the children that would become mine because . . .

I am His.

Part 2

Chapter 8

Innocence

It was thirty-eight years ago that I, a small baby inside my mother's womb, experienced death for the first time.

My grandmother, my mother's mother, went on a trip to Hawaii to escape the torturous Minnesota winter with my uncle and great-grandpa. While there, she started experiencing mysterious symptoms. They came home from their trip early and went straight to the doctor. The diagnosis hit them like a ton of bricks. Brain cancer. They compared the cancer to a strawberry plant with feelers. Surgery was scheduled immediately, and my grandma started radiation and chemotherapy. Her health declined rapidly.

My mom tried desperately to find out the gender of the precious baby she was carrying, but I was stubborn and wouldn't cooperate during the ultrasound. My grandma passed away six months after her diagnosis, while my mom was six months pregnant with me. After time passed, my mom was finally able to go through her mom's closet. As she went past each hanger that held the smell and memory of her mom, she came upon a beautiful white-and-navy Hawaiian dress. Attached was a small white piece of paper with the simple, yet powerful, words written in her mother's handwriting: "For the baby girl." My grandma knew. She already knew.

My sister-in-law recently asked me the moment when I first truly understood death. She waited as I pondered my response and said, "Mine was *The Lion King*. I remember watching it as a young girl and being completely horrified as Mufasa fell to his death. It was so real, and it hit me that he was gone forever."

Your moment will look different from mine. Different from your best friend's, your neighbor's, or a complete stranger's. We lost our children. Some will lose a spouse, their parents, or their closest friends. Or even a pet. But grief is grief. Because grief is love. Don't fight that. And don't compare yours to others. There's not a scale of what loss hurts the worst. Everyone's heart breaks, and a hole replaces what those people or things left behind.

But how you choose to go through the journey is exactly that: your choice. Everyone will process and handle grief in their own way, and none of it is right or wrong.

The dry brown grass crunches under my feet as I walk. The wind is making all the colorful flower petals dance as I pass by. I spread the blanket out in front of the stone etched with the same names that mark my body.

How did we get here? To this place that feels like another home. To this place where a piece of me was buried with you.

Every single day, I see your faces in your siblings. They run wild and free on this earth while you do the same next to Jesus. Oh, the day we will be reunited is something I dream about. How I long to hold your precious faces in my hands and look into your eyes. To feel your touch as you squeeze my hands. To hear your voices call me Mommy.

But for now, as I'm on my knees in prayer, I feel you. Wrapping me in your arms just as Penelope does when she knows I'm sad. She rubs my hand and doesn't even say a word. She misses you too.

As a child, I was scared of my own shadow. Scared to be alone. Scared of the dark. Just scared. Every horror movie that I *never* watched (literally plugged my ears and closed my eyes during previews and commercials) seemed to be set in a dark, eerie cemetery. So obviously, yours truly, was scared of cemeteries. But, after experiencing death firsthand and finding my faith, I can now walk through a cemetery and be at peace rather than have chills run up my spine. We have done a prayer hour in the pitch black, with only the solar lights that loved ones placed near graves guiding our path. If you would have told me years ago that I would be spending my Mother's Day picnicking by a headstone, I would have said you were crazy. But now, every year another Mother's Day rolls around, and we make a day of it.

We go to a local nursery and pick out the season's flowers for the cemetery, carefully mixing and matching colors that will embrace Cohen and Calla's youth. We pack a picnic lunch and set up for an afternoon of eating, planting, and playing. The kids are completely comfortable running past headstones while playing tag. We always make sure to spend a little time at the markers of other family members and close friends, offering up our prayers and love. We aren't afraid to have conversations with our children about death and the significance of where we are. They see my tears, but they see my smiles too.

I don't hide my feelings, but instead, I explain why I am sad so we can talk about Cohen and Calla and pray together. Having my four children in one place fills me up to the brim. All the chaos rolls away, the dust settles, and I can feel all of their love hug my heart.

But I miss the innocence I once possessed. Grief also brought me fear. Once loss hit me straight in my heart; once I was standing over the coffin; once I held the new title of *bereaved mother*—only then did I think this would *ever* happen to me. I believe the naivety was very normal. When it directly impacted my world is when I realized just how delicate life is. I had never experienced the intense pain losing my children filled my body with. It was all-consuming. I have lain crying out to God at our babies' tombstone. I have wished to be taken away from my suffering. I have felt myself fiercely protecting my heart and tiptoeing through times of anxiety and fear. I have part of me here on earth and part of me in heaven. Every part of my being is acutely aware of life's fragility.

Loss completely changed my perspective on life. Don't just get through the days and let life pull you forward. Be in charge of your time and make the choice to be better and do better. I can decide who I give my time to and who I spend it with, because it is truly so precious. I can choose to tell others how I feel and how much love they bring to my life. Share your heart and don't wait. In the blink of an eye, your world can turn upside down, and you won't have any warning. Don't wait for the exact right time or put it off until tomorrow. Push to soak up every moment on earth and relish in each season of life.

I have been through the fire and come out on the other side. Battered and beaten, but I'm here. I am a different person in the aftermath, as I now hold the wisdom of a grieving mother.

I have seen God's goodness amidst my suffering. I have seen God's light through the darkness. I have found comfort in Him through my heartache. I have witnessed God's grace and love firsthand. Therefore, I carry a responsibility to encourage others to look to God and to share what I have received through Him. Our suffering will be someone else's suffering. Others will walk the path we have travelled. I can share the steps we took, the fast lanes, the roadblocks that resulted in detours, the pit stops, and every landmark along the way. Our journey isn't done. And yours surely won't be the exact same. Maybe your GPS has better directions. Free yourself from comparison and settle into the relatability. Breathe in my sweet sorrow, but live your own.

Chapter 9

From Your Knees

Hold your heart steady in Jesus . . .

The air starts to smell of rain. To me, it's the scent of worms making their way to the surface and tossing and turning the dirt around. Everything gets a little heavier. A bit unsettled. Darkness falls. The first few drops hit the pavement . . .

I feel like our world is in a constant impending storm. The thunder and lightning are approaching. The rain is falling. And everyone is distraught and uneasy. We are standing in the wide open, facing overwhelming decisions, uncomfortable conversations, and the complete unknown. All without an umbrella to help withstand the harsh conditions.

We just need to keep walking. Stand tall as the rain hits and keep moving forward. Grace will follow you along the way, as you lead yourself and others home.

God holds the umbrella.

We just need to meet Him.

Prayer

/prer/

A solemn request for help or expression of thanks addressed to God.

A prayer can be simple or complex. Full of grateful praise or an urgency for intervention and grace. No matter how big or small, no matter who says it, whether you are five or eighty-five, whether you're in a room full of people or in the silence of your house, if tears are your words or you can't stop rambling on . . . prayer is powerful.

When the world won't stop spinning enough for you to catch your breath . . . pray.

When your heart constantly searches for reasons and direction but nothing appears . . . pray.

When anger swells and frustration peaks . . . pray.

When the conflicting emotions of motherhood throw themselves at you . . . pray.

When you can no longer stand the weight of your grief . . . pray.

When you feel your kids' hands in your own as they look up to their mommy . . . pray.

When you feel the beauty of your life shining down . . . pray.

When you feel hopeful about tomorrow and your future . . .pray.

Praying is giving yourself to God, wrapping up all of your thoughts and feelings, all of life's best and worst days, all of you, and sending it to up to our Lord. It's not expecting answers, but trusting fully and wholeheartedly that "I am Yours, and You are mine."

Seek a relationship with God. An intimate and sincere one. Spend time with Him. He is the ultimate friend. He is a true confidante and protector of your truth and your sins. He has ears that are always listening, eyes to see you, and a heart that will never withhold love from you.

God is our place of quiet retreat. We need to be still and allow the Lord into our hearts. Tell Him your worries and fears. Let prayer lighten the weight on your shoulders. The amount we all carry was not intended to be carried alone.

As someone who has experienced loss firsthand, I know I have heard the words "Our thoughts and prayers are with you. I will be praying for you . . . " a thousand times. More often than not, this can be a quick expression in an excruciating situation, such as walking through the recession line at a funeral. But recently, I took the time to actually sit back and think on this. Being a prayer warrior is one of the most powerful and giving roles you can take on in this broken world. In the most hopeless situations, God is giving us the power to do something about it. When I was at my lowest point, down in the dirt, dust on my hands and mud in my heart, I prayed. I grasped at His feet desperate for help. You don't always see God working. You may not feel your prayers being acknowledged. But they are heard. Maybe your life needed redirecting, or your safety was threatened, or you needed to get out of your own way—your prayer could have been answered in a way you couldn't see.

Sometimes those words of comfort that make you cringe may also bring the only hope you can cling to. Never turn away prayers. Never minimize how powerful it is to pray for someone besides yourself.

I had a conversation with my sister-in-law about our prayer life. She was pregnant with her sixth baby and overtaken by fear. It consumed her thoughts; she couldn't fight it. She would pray for God's help, but still fear was pulling her under. She thought if she could just hide it, and even pretend it wasn't there, she would have power over it. She prayed to seek relief from the fear, without totally exposing her vulnerability to the Lord. She was ashamed of how she felt and didn't want to be exposed to how He would see her. She was weak and broken but wanted to appear strong and whole. The closer she got to delivery, the worse her fear became. Finally, she was given the most incredible advice. "Sit with the fear. Be still in that moment and feel those feelings. No words need to be said . . . just be. Just be you with Christ."

Something shifted in her; it felt like for the first time in her life she *truly* prayed. She was so afraid He wouldn't love her in that weak place. But in reality, meeting Him exactly where she was formed the most intimate connection and she was overtaken by the Holy Spirit. Where she felt messy and lost and broken, He gave her peace.

We must allow the Holy Spirit to work through us as we dive deeper into our relationship with God. Speak out about temptations and desires. Share your struggles and fears. Satan doesn't revel in our pain, but in God's anguish. I don't want to give Satan too much power. He rejoices in us moving away from God. So when we hide away and feel ashamed of what we have done or where our minds may have wandered, Satan attacks our vulnerability and confusion. Instead of running from what scares us or what we don't understand, we need to speak to God. Confess your sins and surrender to His will. Release the weight of shame and anxiety. God knows exactly what you are going to tell Him—and the most beautiful part, He still listens. Explore every aspect of this powerful connection, this friendship that God has placed in your hands. There is no room for Satan to enter our hearts if the space holds Jesus. Fill your soul with God's word and prayer so it can't be filled with anxiety and worry. Temptations seek those openings. We must seek His truth instead of bending truth to justify our imperfect feelings. Our feelings are what our minds perceive. We should ask God to transform our feelings into the truth.

Show others who God is. Embrace what brings you closer to Jesus and reject what pulls you away. Don't rely on the opinions of others when living for God and God alone.

Leaning into God and a life filled with His word can be an overwhelming journey. It can make me feel hesitant and nervous. But my mind and body are often craving that relationship with our Heavenly Father. So where do I start, and where can you if you feel that way too?

Speak.

Speak the words that are in your heart. He is listening. Are the words not formed? God is still listening. Through your tears, He hears you. Give yourself space to immerse yourself in Him. Free up some of your crowded mind to let Him in. Chaos surrounds our lives, but we must not fall. God can make miracles. He can move mountains and cure sickness. But something as simple as a bad day can make us forget all that. We need to continue to listen, even in God's silence. He is working. He is making good. His silence doesn't mean absence. He makes us walk when we want to run, sit still when we want to move, and wait when we want it now. He is building something beautiful in our hurt. We may wonder why the struggle and heartache exist. We must walk through the hardships to become what God has intended for us to be. God does not want perfection. Perfection is unattainable. He is just seeking our surrendered hearts.

A meaningful and sincere prayer life can be daunting. I still can get intimidated by the thought of it. Prayer is not for show. It is communication between me and the Lord. I find the best ways to spend time with God and to actively pray are to have a thankful heart, be open and honest with my true feelings, and be still. I mean literally, be still. Remove all distractions and be present with the Lord. Set aside time in your day to give Him your complete attention. Listen fully and open your heart up to hearing Him. Praise Him for what He has brought into your life. Ask Him what you feel you need: strength, healing, comfort. But also pray for others. Seek forgiveness for wrongdoings and forgive those who have hurt you. Release the pain and the weight of others' opinions. Pray for God's will to be done. All that matters to us, even if it may seem trivial, is important to God because we are important to God.

"A bridge is a structure built to span a physical obstacle . . . usually something that is otherwise difficult or impossible to cross."

—WIKIPEDIA

I need to cross that bridge, but the path is cluttered with debris. There are people criticizing and judging the direction I'm going. Did I take the wrong turn? Is this the right way? It is too steep and too dangerous. I don't feel equipped to make the trek. I'm not ready. It's not the right time. It feels impossible, and I'm only me.

Yes, yes, yes. But . . .

The bridge between sin and forgiveness is Jesus. The bridge between shame and acceptance is Jesus. The bridge between heartache and hope is Jesus. The bridge between here and eternity is Jesus. Jesus is our bridge to God. Jesus gave us access. God is who will hold us up over treacherous landscapes and darkened pathways. He will be our foundation through raging pain and hurt. He will give us hope in our hearts when all hope seems lost. God never said life wouldn't be a battle. We are humans in a weakened and shattered world. But, as our Lord and Savior, He promised He will battle with us.

Choosing your faith first can be extremely challenging. Being lax in your spiritual life can oftentimes feel easier, with less pressure. But that freedom of doing what you want without caring about God can lead to superficial connections, feelings of shame, judgmental thoughts, meaningless days, and a path toward making wrong decisions. Concentrate on the Lord. Satan knows our vices and weaknesses. He will grab ahold of the smallest string.

Chase that hunger for Jesus. Fill up the empty spaces with His word and teachings. Start your days talking to God, rather than clutching comparison amid the darkness of social media. Let Him untangle all the knots of worry; let Him give you rest. Let His presence settle into your bones. Feel the freedom He provides to sing His praises. Search the world, finding His beauty at every turn.

It can be easier to believe in God without pursuing God. You can pray behind closed doors and keep yourself hidden in the back pews of the church. Religion is a hard topic. It has broken up marriages and families, and even torn countries apart. I was at a crossroads, choosing between a very dark path or the hand outstretched to me. Praise the Lord, I followed my heart. I want to learn more, filling my mind with knowledge and my body with the Holy Spirit. I need to not be afraid or ashamed of my love for our Heavenly Father. I want others to know and see that love.

What if you don't have anyone to turn to? What if your support system is nonexistent? What if you just don't know what to do next?

I get it. Grief throws you in a tailspin and then you have to figure out which way is up. I don't have all the answers. The path Luke and I took was how *we* got here. But it is going to be different for everyone. If you are feeling lost, please know there is no handbook.

Not that you need it from me, but I give you permission to take that next step. Sometimes you aren't just taking grief day by day. You are taking it hour by hour, minute by minute, breath by breath. Remember, you are *never* alone.

Here are a few options that may help:

- If you are in the hospital, talk to your nurse or the hospital social worker. They have tons of resources. Even if you aren't ready now, take the information, because you never know when the right time will come.

- Find grief support groups local to your area. If you aren't prepared for face-to-face meetings yet, search online. There are a lot of Facebook groups to join.

- Look for different ways to express your feelings when you don't have the words to say aloud. Open up a journal and release it all. My writing opened up wounds that I unconsciously wasn't allowing to the surface, and it was incredibly healing. Your thing could be music or painting or drawing. Be creative.

- Many therapists specialize in grief/trauma. Take advantage of their knowledge and unbiased perspective to share the weight you are carrying.

- If you don't belong to a church, please know that you can still walk into or even call one. Whether they can help you there or lead you to the right place, they are still there.

Most of all, don't try to do this alone. You aren't meant to.

Chapter 10

Bloom

Tiny seeds are planted. Roots find their home in the black dirt. Stems search for the warmth of the sun. Buds bloom and then petals fall. Some stretch and grow, while others wilt and wither.

Flowers unapologetically show the world their journey. They are not afraid to let us witness each step of the process— all the pretty, the in-between, and even the end.

As I ramble on throughout this book, you may be thinking, *This girl talks a lot about God and prayer and healing. She tells us the steps she took and the progress she's made. But she doesn't seem okay. Is her faith helping her? Is prayer helping her? Is her God really helping her?*

I get it. I don't have it all together. On top of my grief, I am still a struggling human. I have anxiety. I get lost in comparisons. I have good days and bad days. And I can say with every ounce of my being I am strongly and openly broken. I won't pretend that isn't the case. I do, however, find it brave to live with such loss and grief and still find beauty and happiness along the way. I would not—I repeat—I would not be where I am without God. I want to tell people who He is. I want to scream it from the mountaintops. When you read this, I want you to feel how much I love Jesus. When you choose to follow the Lord, life doesn't simply get easy. It's not all rainbows and butterflies. But it is extremely humbling to know that even when you're down in the dumps, at the end of your rope, at rock bottom, God will always choose you. Knowing our every sin, flaw, and fault, he still chooses us. His mercy remains.

Yes, I have a beautiful, happy family, full of smiling faces and incredible memories. I also have a deep pain that coexists. And that is exactly it: these things coexist. My grief does not define who I am, but it is a huge part of my story. But God *is* my story. And He isn't going anywhere. We are not promised a life without pain. We will have seasons of unrest and seasons of waiting. We endure heartache and suffering. In all of those things, however, we are shown why faith is so necessary. Believing in God gives me a solid ground to walk on when all too often I feel unsteady and unable to find a firm grasp on reality. My faith provides not only a beautiful foundation, but a safe place to rest. A haven of comfort and never-ending support and devotion. It allows me to walk with Jesus, value the life He has given me, focus my attention, and set my gaze on heaven.

Life is short. This we all know.

In my time here—all the seconds, minutes, hours, days, and years—I will strive to:

- Continue building my intimate relationship with God. I want to read His word and consume myself with more prayer time, both alone and with my husband and kids. I want to learn and grow in my faith. God has my back. While others may run from the raw and rough edges of my life, God embraces them. God saved *me* a seat. God wants *me* on His team. God chose *me*. You have never been gone too long to come back to Him. Pray with any amount of faith you have inside. He can handle whatever you throw at him, and He will be listening and waiting with the most gracious understanding you can imagine.

- Embrace my roles as a mother and wife. I want to love on my family and be completely present. In all the big and all the small. Embrace the chaos, because it will slip away into silence before I know it. In my hard seasons of motherhood, I can have the desire to wish time away. But if I take a step back and look at the bigger picture, I know there will be an abundance of "hard seasons," whether I am the sleep-deprived brand-new parent of an infant, the constantly worried parent of a reckless teenager, the praying empty-nester parent of a child leaving home for the first time, or a child transitioning from being taken care of to taking care of her parents. The seasons will change as time passes, and there will always be that "hard," but I don't want to miss out on all the good in between. I want to sincerely realize that these two roles are far from inconsequential and will always be the most important and beautiful to me. The longer I live and the harder I fight for peace and contentment in my life, the more I crave positive and life-giving relationships. I want to surround myself with the good. I want people who not only are in my corner, but also challenge me and push me to be my best.

- Allow boredom to exist in my life. To just "be still." Connect with my friends and family face to face. Have real, honest relationships without a screen separating us. It's too easy to pick up my phone and scroll through the infinite world of social media, or to jump on the latest binge-worthy TV series. I'm 100 percent guilty of feeling the need to be distracted. Sitting on my phone while watching TV—no commercials, no waiting . . . ever. Instant gratification is our reality now. But setting down the remote and putting away my phone is allowing myself to be bored. In turn, I can be still and listen. I need to quit trying to listen for God in the loudness, when He can be waiting in the silence.

- Rejoice in all God has blessed my life with and honor Him in all I am and do. To step away from the hate, separation, comparison, anger, bullying, insensitivity . . . and step into paying it forward, kindness, bravery, compassion, living, and love. I am a complex person. I would consider myself a needy soul. I ask for a lot, and I ask often. However, I try to give just as much back to the world. I hurt when others hurt. I weep when they weep. I am a true empath. Reach out to those you love and those you know need it most. Lead by example through including others, meeting in the middle, and orienting your heart toward love. Be the mom who isn't afraid of being different, who isn't afraid of being herself. That may mean holding an unpopular role outside of today's "normal." And that's okay.

"So let Him unravel your worry-woven tapestry. Let Him cut it down to nothing more than severing threads. Let Him remind you that in the unraveling of all the things you had planned, He was only paving the way toward a beautiful woven God-ordained future up ahead."

—MORGAN HARPER NICHOLS,
Christian musician and writer

Do you ever feel like you are right back in the middle school cafeteria, all alone at a table, desperately hoping others will join you?

Or are you sitting in class as the teacher calls out, "Pick a partner!" and feeling your heart sink in your chest?

Or are you at the playground as kids are gathering on the field for a game of kickball, and . . . well, you know the rest.

In all of these situations, we are looking for solidarity. For a team. For community. For belonging.

I was there. Fast-forward, and I am now thirty-eight years old and still yearning to fit in. I consume myself with wanting the validation and approval of others. What does that even mean?

Well, to me, it means I am the perfect mom. The one who does all the right things and makes it look really natural and simple, but on top of that is still really cool and fun. I set unrealistically high expectations for myself, attempting to balance being an impeccable wife, daughter, sister, and friend, and possibly even doing some self-care along the way. I need to help others and make time for everyone. I need to show the importance of every one of my relationships and not let one soul feel left out. I need to read the Bible, exercise five times a week, throw that face mask on, meal plan and prep, start a book club, and gosh darn it, just keep my children alive.

Ugh. Just writing that was exhausting.

God is all-knowing. He knows us beyond our proudest moments. He sees the ugly truths behind what we post on social media. He is not surprised that you are disappointed in Him when things did not unfold like you had planned. Our very own dreams crumbled in front of us, breaking every ounce of power and control we thought we possessed. We don't need to hide away and tell others our burdens. We do not need to protect God from our thoughts and feelings; we need to bring them to Him. God isn't waiting for us to mess up. He already *knows* we will. We are imperfect human beings. We are sinners. Allow yourself to be free of trying to exemplify His impossible holiness. Instead, surrender completely so He can love you where you are at. Turn to God. Ask Him to show you His way, not your own. Believe in the beauty and truth of His word and His love.

Find stillness to just be. To deeply feel emotions and not justify them. Our feelings do not define us, but how we act upon them does. I have spent years defending how I feel according to what I think society expects. I try to sabotage my heart and what God made it to be.

People often ask me for advice when someone they know is grieving. We were right there in the thick of grief and know what was and was not helpful. Do I wish I was knowledgeable in this area? Absolutely not. But God chose us to be the parents to two powerful and serene saints in heaven. This is our story. Witnessing our journey, as we transparently walk through it, could be all someone needs to push forward.

"Trust in the Lord with all your heart, on your own intelligence do not rely; in all your ways be mindful of him, and he will make straight your paths."

—PROVERBS 3:5–6

God wants us to share our stories with the world, but we have to take the first step in telling them. A lot of times, Luke and I start talking about our journey and end up talking about how good God is. None of it makes sense. But our job isn't to make sense of it; it is to trust God and His plan for us.

I want you to embrace your broken and speak your truth. I want you to tell the world your story. But I also ask that you settle in and live that story. I struggle trying to save the world but forget that I need saving too.

When moments of grief start to rise and surge through your body like a bull chasing a matador, you may want to run from your feelings. We run from the bull. You must choose to face these emotions and stand up and fight—but with grace for your mind and body. Sometimes the fight may mean an hour of therapy. A chat with a friend. Prayer time alone. Or saying their names aloud. When we choose not to tell our stories or share anxious thoughts with God, we are potentially missing the chance to allow our wounds to heal others. We are avoiding obstacles that could be paths to joy. God loves to turn broken things into beautiful things. Don't try to run and hide from the broken.

We grow in the trenches. In the dirt, we dig deeper roots.

Life doesn't stop when trauma wrecks your world. The earth keeps spinning, even when you feel you are spinning ten times faster. The pages in your book of life still turn, the months move one into the next, and the sparrows fly in every season. Whether it is spring, summer, fall, or winter, the birds take their next flight.

If you look close enough, everyone you see is hiding a degree of pain under their smiles. They are standing on a mountain of insecurities, overwhelm, and the chaos of the crazy world we live in. There will be sorrow and there will be loss. Everyone will experience death in one way or another. Death is a part of our mortal existence.

While we know that everyone experiences death, we don't know each story. We don't know how a person's day has gone or what they're thinking. Delivering the simple question of "When are the babies coming?" to a couple or the teasing statement of "It's about time!" to your newly pregnant cousin could drop them right where they stand. When a person has held countless negative pregnancy tests, found out she has PCOS (polycystic ovary syndrome), or simply cannot fathom losing another baby, a "harmless" comment is awful to hear. It's not intentional, but we don't walk in everyone's shoes. That person could be miscarrying as you're speaking to her. Or she just left a dreadful doctor's appointment with heart-wrenching bad news. We do not know. We must acknowledge that life doesn't always go according to plan. Choose to live with gentle hands, careful words, and a kind heart when you encounter others.

When something traumatic happens in our lives, it can feel like we are the only ones who have gone through this or are truly heartbroken.

But everyone has something. Everyone suffers. Trauma is just part of our fallen world. If we unite and uncover our scars, we can rise above and heal together. We can learn to live with that hurt while embracing the joy waiting for us . . . together. We are not meant to live alone. We are creatures who crave connection and community. If we open ourselves up, if we remove the veil, if we take away the stigma, if we know our worth and share our truth, I think we will all find that others cannot only benefit but find it relatable and comforting.

I remember walking across the street from the hospital to McDonald's for lunch. It was almost a surreal experience to see normal life happening around me. People hustling to the drive-thru on their hurried lunch breaks, kids meeting for conversations in the booth next to us, a mom with her screaming toddler who desperately wanted ice cream. My world was less than 200 yards away in the NICU, fighting for their lives in small, sterile incubators, and this was happening outside. Life was continuing to move around me.

It's been ten years since the last time I held them in my arms. I can still feel the weight of them. I can still see every detail of their beautiful faces. I can still feel my heart being torn from my chest as the casket closed.

Grief doesn't leave you because love doesn't leave you. Grief is love. It's just love that has made its home in your heart. This loss is love that I want to continue holding onto. Feeling that pain or remembering that particular smell brings them into my present, even though heaven and earth are what separate us.

Why can we so freely give others grace and fill them up with love and compassion, but can't do the same for ourselves?

There are days I wake up full of anxiety. I have a tight chest, pounding heart, and moments where I can't catch my breath. My anxiety comes in like a freight train but is unsteady like a roller coaster. I can't predict it, and sometimes it sneaks in far too quickly.

There are times I'm ashamed of it. I feel like a letdown to my kids, to my husband, to my family. I beat myself up about being a bad friend. Then the anxiety compounds and I spiral into loads of self-doubt and feelings of inadequacy. I try to fight against it. I get angry at myself—why can't I just get it together and be "normal"?

There are days I yell at my kids. I get impatient and short-tempered. I scroll on my phone too long or I make my phone a priority over them. I don't always have the energy or desire to play with them. The guilt that follows is draining and it takes its toll on me. I've lost children that I won't ever be able to play with. Why am I taking my kids for granted? Why am I allowing my "feelings" to take precedence over being a mom?

Our minds can play tricks on us, and our feelings can fluctuate like the temperature outside or the stock market. I am incredibly guilty of getting in my own head and telling myself lies. But they aren't my lies; they are the Evil One's. I must rely on the Truth. His Truth. God gave humans "feelings" to be relational. Emotions help us live in healthy relationships and stay connected to God and others. They exist to tell us something. But Satan plants seeds of disbelief and uncertainty, which create those lies of doubt, fear, and worry. I was created by His hand to be unique and extraordinary. I need to accept all my flaws and faults for what they are: normal. I am human. Life doesn't always make sense. Well, to be honest, most of the time it doesn't. I think humans try to take control and pave our way through this world. We must understand that we aren't that powerful. God has us all wrapped in His arms. We have to stop trying to escape Him. We are peeling out of His grasp instead of accepting His embrace. We will continuously fight against the current. God created us with reckless love and such a powerful purpose. God knows all, and He never lies. Live in His Truth, not in your feelings. This is one of the most difficult things for me to do. I get overtaken by my emotions and feed into Satan's attacks. Pray and know that Jesus is loving you and fighting for you.

"I praise you, because I am wonderfully made; wonderful are your works! My very self you know. My bones are not hidden from you, When I was being made in secret, fashioned in the depths of the earth. Your eyes saw me unformed; in your book all are written down; my days were shaped, before one came to be."

—PSALM 139:14–16

Chapter 11

Ways to Remember Those We Will Never Forget

God-Moments

God hung the moon and placed the stars. He created the ground we walk on and the hands we hold. He designed us in His beautiful image, knowing exactly who we would become. Until I grew in my relationship with the Lord, and truly leaned into Him, the God-moments were invisible to me but present. Coincidences are not coincidences. He doesn't design accidents; He creates purposes. In our time here on earth, God is near and ever present. We just have to look for Him.

I completely believe that God uses objects as signs pointing to Him. These are personal encounters where God's presence and love are revealed. Some people may find pennies in their path, cardinals at their bird feeder, or feathers in the wind. I feel so much through music and song.

The number two is one of our God-moments. It conveys the meaning of a union; between husband and wife, between Christ and the church, 1 + 1 equals 2. Luke and I were married on February 2. The twins were due on November 2, but joined us on July 2. Cohen passed away two days later. Calla passed away on July 22. Cohen and Calla are twins—two of a kind, a perfect pair. Two continues to show up just when we need it.

God also plants people in our lives—those who will help us grow and build to be our best selves. These people God places right where we need them most. Some people will come in and move out quickly, but still make an impact. Some people are toxic and have to be pushed out, but may have taught us something. And some are forever.

I thank these people, from the bottom of my heart, for being the shelter that allows my soul to unfold and be free. To be who I am and feel how I feel. And to be loved without end. They may not even know the depth of my love and appreciation for them, but they all impacted my life and changed it for the better.

I had just delivered Cohen and Calla and was being whisked down to the operating room for surgery. Before we left the room, our priest, Father Eric, came through my door. He asked if he could pray over me. I don't think I actually answered, but I must have attempted a small nod. I lay there silently weeping, in shock and pain, overcome with fear. He began to speak. The words rushed over every part of me. It seemed that time had come to a halt. In that particular moment, I felt overwhelming peace envelop my trembling body and anxious mind. I was extremely grateful for Father Eric and his comfort, but I was completely unaware of what was truly happening. Looking back, in the place I am now with my faith, I realize that as Father Eric's words settled over me, there was Jesus. My Jesus, sitting by my side, covering me with grace and protection. I can envision His hand wrapping around mine, taking my fears from me. I always imagine my Grandpa's hands when I think of Jesus's hands. They were masculine, strong, well-worn hands that showed the hardworking life he lived. But they were also somehow so soft and always felt calm, steady, and sure. Jesus pulled me close and showed me just how big God loves. One of the biggest God-moments of my life.

Tattoos

They aren't for everyone. I never had one before our loss. I was terrified of needles and could never decide what I wanted. The twins' original due date was coming up, and we wanted to do something special to commemorate it. So, on November 2, 2013, I got *Cohen and Calla* tattooed on my forearm in a delicate and feminine font. Feeling the pain of the needle penetrating my skin was a tangible way to hold onto them in that moment.

Eight years later, the lyric "You grow Your roses on my barren soul" from my favorite band NEEDTOBREATHE, accompanied by wild roses, found its way onto my other arm.

Wild roses. Rooted deep into the earth, grasping onto the soil, filling up with the nutrients and water provided, which are always just enough to help them bloom.

We were given rose bushes after the twins' funeral by our dear friends. The bushes have survived multiple transplants, one full winter in a basement tub with no nurturing, and my complete lack of a green thumb. They have withstood every element and stayed with us. For over ten years.

No matter the hardships, or how wounded you may feel, your poor, lost, empty soul can still grow powerful and mighty because of our Lord Jesus Christ. Our Heavenly Father takes the broken and makes them beautiful. He turns darkness into light, hate into love, and hopeless into hopeful.

So I marked down four roses on my very own barren soul—one big, one small, and two that never blossomed but became saints in their Father's house.

Traditions

Holidays, anniversaries, and birthdays are so important. If your mother or brother or daughter is turning another year older, you do your best to make their day special. We hang colorful streamers from their doorways, send them flowers, and sing our best version of "Happy Birthday" to make them feel loved and appreciated. I believe that most of us would feel sad or let down if our day were forgotten. Yes, I believe we should acknowledge and celebrate how important someone is to us *every* day of the year. Yes, I believe holidays and birthdays can become commercialized. But I also believe that someone you love has every right to be recognized on a special day. I feel the same way about my children in heaven. I hope and pray that others remember them too. Why do I want that? Why do

I need others to share in my hurt as I grieve for my children? Why do I need them to sit alongside me in my pain? I want to celebrate my children. I want to say their names and blow out their birthday candles. I want to remember them for the love and light they brought into our world. But that is going to include tears and sadness. I guess I need for others to acknowledge that my grief will never leave me. Because, again, that love will never leave me.

Our traditions keep memories alive. We mindfully choose to celebrate the milestones of our twins in our family, and we involve them in our lives.

The year we lost Cohen and Calla, when Christmas was fast approaching, I dug through the seasonal red tub, moving aside tree decorations in search of our stockings. There were only two. Husband and wife. It was so empty, so bare. My dreams of what could have been were replaced by the brutal gaps above the fireplace. Before I completely self-imploded, my incredible mom came to the rescue, presenting us with matching plaid stockings for the entire family. The mantel was now complete. But then came the traumatic thought of never seeing their stockings filled with toys on Christmas morning. And that started another tradition.

I needed to say their names with our family, no matter what that looked like. I needed to have them present, even though they weren't there. I turned on my computer and opened a new document, a letter to the twins' grandparents and Godparents, asking them to write something to the twins for us to open on Christmas morning. It could be anything, really . . . Tell them about your lives, thank them for theirs, draw a picture, or simply write a "Merry Christmas." I anxiously opened the mailbox, praying to see those letters addressed to our dear Cohen and Calla. We received so many the first year. The tradition continues to this day. The letters are much fewer, but just as beautiful. It has allowed us to take the time to soak in their memories, say their names aloud, and still see their stockings "full" on that precious Christmas morning.

Several years ago, we were blessed to celebrate the twins' birthday with our family. We captured beautiful innocence and so much love as we shared our words on floating lanterns. As we were each writing our notes, the kids wanted to join in. Penelope wrote her cute little backward *P* on both lanterns. Some did hearts and signed their name with the cutest messy handwriting. Then my nephew, Keegan, took my breath away. He started drawing, completely focused. Everyone asked what he was drawing and he just kept saying, "You'll know." He finished, and his dad asked what it was. He replied, "The gates of heaven."

The lanterns were finally lit and flying high. I asked Penelope where she thought they were going. Without hesitation, she said, "They're going to Cohen and Calla, Mommy. They will make them so happy. Then maybe they'll come home because we miss them so much." The tears fell, and she wiped them away and kissed me. Her grace showed me God . . . that He is our Savior.

Rock Painting

One summer, we were camping in Wisconsin and I was watching the kiddos at the playground. We noticed a vividly colored rock sitting in with all the natural stones. Someone had painted it bright pink, with the simple message "Be Happy" in sunshine yellow. It got me thinking and, in turn, I researched more about these painted rocks. People had started placing them throughout their towns for others to find. You could put them anywhere and hope someone will see them and it will brighten their day. You can either rehide them for someone else to find or keep them for yourself.

When we got home from our trip, we were on the hunt for rocks of our own to paint. Well, with the help of other "rock painters," we learned that the shores of Lake Superior in Duluth, Minnesota, hold the mother lode of perfectly flat and beautiful painting rocks.

We have painting sessions at home. They involve about twenty minutes of the kids chaotically throwing paint on some rocks—*all* the colors—usually too much, where it drips off the edges and takes over twenty-four hours to dry. Then, there's a collective sigh as they say they are done, followed by an after-bedtime therapy session of Mom transforming the rocks into ones we can share with the world. A small *CC* is placed on the outside of each rock to always remember our babes.

The kids love "hiding" the rocks, mostly at campgrounds in the summer, where they are continuously checking to see if old rocks are still there or if someone finally found them. I highly recommend this fun way to celebrate with the whole family.

Support Groups/Organizations

After the twins passed, we went through the funeral planning in a fog. I actually don't remember much of it at all. We chose music and picked a casket and made picture boards. I find it almost impossible to make decisions under that sort of numbing pain cloud. This is why you must surround yourself with the right people, the people who know your heart. Also, the professionals. The funeral home directors were incredible. The church surrounded us with so much love and took care of all the details. Our priests, our parents, our siblings, and friends—so many people showed up.

And also, IRIS: Infants Remembered In Silence. They are a "non-profit organization that is dedicated to offering support, education and resources to parents, families, friends and professionals on the death of a child in early pregnancy (miscarriage, ectopic pregnancy, molar pregnancy, etc.) or from stillbirth, premature birth, neo-natal death, birth defects, sudden infant death syndrome (SIDS), illness, accidents, and all other types of infant & early childhood death."

Diana, the owner and founder of IRIS, is incredible. As a bereaved mother herself, she just gets it. She is kind and gentle, but also courageous and strong. Her heart of gold is visible to all who meet her. She is such a blessing to our family and our community.

IRIS's advocate program is "designed to assist parents from the time that they have found out that their child has died, through delivery, in the hours following delivery, and through the funeral. Advocates assist parents with a variety of services, including explaining delivery options, acting as a doula (labor coach), assisting with creating precious keepsakes and memories. This includes bathing and dressing the baby, to taking a variety of pictures, taking hand and foot prints, castings and much more. On an average an IRIS Advocate will spend 8–12 hours working with a family in the hospital setting and/or 4–6 hours working with a child in the funeral home setting."

All of the things that we wouldn't have thought about, or didn't have the physical energy or mental processing to do, IRIS did.

IRIS doesn't stop supporting and loving on families after the initial time of loss. They provide so many resources and events to attend to remember the children gone from our arms but forever remaining in our hearts.

The IRIS Turkey Trot has become such a special event for our family. Every year on Thanksgiving morning, thousands of people gather to walk or run a 5k/10k. On a day made for counting your blessings and giving thanks, we celebrate and honor the beautiful souls who left this earth too soon. To survive the brutal Minnesota winters, we bundle up in all our gear to face varying degrees of weather. We have endured freezing rain, billowing gusts of wind, pounding snow, and beautiful sun.

The November following the dreadful July we lost the twins, we stepped onto that pavement with tears in our eyes. We were surrounded by so many parents and families who had similarly lost their children, but all with their own unique stories. We could feel the love, empathy, and understanding as we took each step. The first year after, we started loading our baby girl into the stroller, wrapped like a little burrito to protect her from the weather. During COVID, we walked the "trot" on our own due to its cancellation. This past year we had our two kids walking with us as we braved the 3.1 miles.

About halfway through, the route turns onto a walking path behind a neighborhood of houses. My heart always skips a beat and I feel my breath start to quicken. The path is lined with signs holding the names and pictures of babies who are gone but never forgotten. Prayers stream through my mind as the teardrops fall like rain. Down by this path, I have been embraced by my husband, linked arms with my sisters, held the hand of my mother, and cuddled my own kids. We round the bend, and their names sear my eyes. In that moment, I am overcome by emotions. All the emotions. Gratefulness, longing, happiness, grief. But I am allowed to feel that. The entire community is allowed to feel their feelings and be comforted and supported, while raising money for an amazing organization. It is an incredibly beautiful event to witness and be a part of.

It took me six years after losing Cohen and Calla to finally step out of my comfort zone, and my immediate safety net, and agree to go to a grief retreat. I was referred to Faith's Lodge in Danbury, Wisconsin, while we were still in the hospital with the twins. I put it on the back burner at that time, and it pretty much fell off the stovetop as the years passed by. But God knows what He is doing. In 2019, as I was going through a memory tub for one of the twins, I found the Faith's Lodge brochure. There are options for the entire family to be a part of these retreats, for all types of losses. I researched it online and found a weekend retreat available in the fall of 2019 for bereaved mothers. I booked it that day. I needed to do it on my own.

I was so anxious on the drive there, questioning why I would have ever done this to myself. *Maybe I should just turn around. I'm not ready.* But then I saw the sign tucked in the trees: "Faith's Lodge – A Place Where Hope Grows." *Oh, my heart.*

The location was serene, a beautiful wooded area with gorgeous fall colors of golds, oranges, and reds surrounding the entire acreage. The log house fit perfectly. I walked in and immediately felt a sense of peace. Everyone gets their own room, which is named in honor of a child in heaven. I will always remember my room: Brandon's Suite. He was a beautiful baby boy, who passed after less than three months on earth. I found it so special to have someone to intentionally pray for when I sat down on the cozy bed in my room.

There were six of us. All mothers of babies or children lost. We had very different backgrounds and very different stories, but we all had the very unique bond of being bereaved moms. The connection was so concrete and remarkable. I found it incredibly freeing to be able to share all about Cohen and Calla, the ups and downs and even some of the things I didn't dare share with anyone else. No one questioned or judged. We laughed and cried and just sat in the silence with one another. We prayed and shared and loved. It was an experience that I will always be grateful for. I hold every mother there in a very special place in my heart.

Chapter 12

The Golden Rule

When I was a child, I never understood adults.

When I was a student, I never understood teachers.

When I was single, I never understood marriage.

When I was kid-free, I never understood parents.

When I was innocent, I never understood death.

There is nothing wrong with being on the other side of life. We must reach deep into our hearts for anyone on the opposite end of our worlds. Our minds, bodies, and spirits are only fully known and comprehended by the Lord. So, our role as humans is to share kindness, compassion, respect, patience, understanding, and unending love, even if we do not understand.

If you have never lost a child, I ask that you pray for every person who has. I have witnessed it in my family, my tribe, my town. I have held babies who took their last breaths in my arms.

I will never make sense of it, but I do know with all my heart that God didn't want them to die. He doesn't ever want for our babies and children to die. Our earthly home holds tragedy, impossible situations, and unimaginable evil. Because of medical and physical reasons, Cohen and Calla came prematurely. Their hearts and lungs were not fully developed.

Maybe God saved them from a life of suffering.

My twins' purpose was far beyond what our earthly home could hold. I was made to be their mother. I will share their story and shout their names from the highest mountains.

Their presence envelops my existence.

Everything I do involves their beautiful souls. I feel my purpose was to give light to this darkness. To help others find hope through the heartache. To give mothers and fathers the space to grieve and hold onto their children. To show our culture that a baby is always a miracle and always remembered. To never stop believing in our powerful God and the heavens that await us in eternity.

Please remember, you never know someone's story.

You haven't walked in their footsteps.

You haven't held their smiles or cried their tears.

Grief can be like a storm, coming without warning. You find yourself unprepared to battle the crushing winds. You get lost in the torrential rainfall and feel your calls for help are lost in the thunder. You search far off into the oblivion for signs of life, desperately waiting to feel the sun on your skin. The clouds eventually part and the sun comes out again. But if you look, you can see the next storm in the distance.

The journey of grief is exhausting, strenuous, and lifelong. The storms do get lighter and gentler, and spread out to become more sporadic, but the dark clouds never stop forming.

I believe society puts a certain amount of pressure on those who have just suffered any sort of heartache, trauma, or sadness. Immediately, our hearts seek to comfort and protect these people. Then, naturally, because we are human, we put ourselves in their shoes and suffer right alongside them. There is a certain amount of pity for them, and even feeling thankful that it didn't happen to us. How awful does that sound? But it's the truth.

Eventually, much quicker than one may expect, life goes on for the rest of us. Routines settle back in and everyday life presses forward. The person grieving is expected to "move on."

It can become very isolating and lonely to be in that position. You can almost force this expected "moving on" by putting on a smile and pushing the feelings under the surface. But nothing is healing and the pain of ignoring it is excruciating. The thought of pretending those lost didn't exist or that their impact on your heart was miniscule can cause you to dig yourself far down into a hole of misery.

Everyone tells the grieving, "You're so strong." But I think we need to reconsider how we view strength. Sometimes that "strength" is covering up the hurt beneath the surface. What is really under there? What mask are you putting on to cover the sadness with a smile? I believe sharing what is hurting is the strongest thing you can do.

It pains us to see others hurting, so our intuition says to give them advice, find a solution, and "fix" it. (I am this person. I have a huge tendency to help fix whatever is wrong.) If they just make a plan and follow through with it, we can all pretend this never happened. Instead, we should console them in their times of need. Most of the time, rest and comfort are essential.

This is where we need to love the grieving where they are at. Allow them to be broken. Give them the space and time they need. Fill them up with love, but not just some of the time. Be aware of their feelings and emotions and, of course, keep them safe. But don't force them to forget. Help them to remember.

Grief and trauma are very complex. To explain the feelings that rush back to me so quickly and sometimes so unexpectedly is impossible. I'll have days on end where I cry for reasons I can't explain. I then wrap myself in self-doubt, embarrassment, and a constant struggle of being ashamed of my grief. The conflicting emotions of putting on a happy face while I feel anything but happy on the inside are at times too much to bear. My mind searches through each situation for worry. Every single role I play is deeply examined and finely criticized. I avoid reality by isolating myself in the safety of my home, shutting out the rest of the world. Any plans or appointments on my calendar can make my heart race. I start mindlessly eating and lack motivation or energy. I can't sleep, even though I'm utterly exhausted. I know what I need to do, but I can't force my mind or body to do it. Pray. Exercise. Call someone. Pray again. Meditate. Take a bath. Write in my journal. Do breathing exercises. Get good sleep. Eat healthily. And, finally, pray again.

Then there is the aftermath of guilt: my short temper with my kids, missing out on events with friends or family, knowing I need to embrace every single second of my precious life. I worry far too much about what others think. I get consumed with wanting to be the best person I can as a wife, mother, daughter, sister, friend, and then feel as if I have disappointed in all roles.

But I keep pushing forward. I make it to the next day, then the next. Mostly due to my tribe: my husband, my kids, my mom and dad, my best friends. If they only knew how they help me every single day. I try to focus on the beauty of my life. Breathe in life, exhale worry. The "moments" pass and I get back on track. I try to let my soul rest in Jesus. Find happiness by choosing yourself and your family first.

When life is smooth and good news is abundant, it is much easier to praise God and tell of His great love. When life is threatening and shortcomings are plentiful, we lose hope in our Savior.

Satan is knocking on the door. He attacks us during chaos and confusion, when we are fearful and anxious. He sneaks in and finds ways to tempt us and pull us away from our true beliefs.

When we are at our lowest, feeling heartache, pain, anger, frustration, fear, or neglect, this is the time to reach out to God. Don't hide away in silence. Lay your brokenness at His feet. Lean into Him more than ever. Show even more grace to others, because that is probably when they need it most. Keep searching for the good in people. Be patient, understanding, generous, and compassionate. Love your family and spread kindness everywhere you go. Focus on the little things that you can control, and let God take care of the big things.

Even when it hurts, now and always, trust and love Jesus.

It can be as simple as seeing a pregnant mom. Or any twins or multiples. Going to the doctor's office. The first day of school.

Anniversaries. Birthdays. Christmas morning. Our babies' milestones. Cardinals. The month of July. The number two.

Triggers can make themselves known quickly and unexpectedly. I can be completely aware of them and they'll still hit just as hard. They can be small tugs at my heartstrings or full-blown panic attacks. The feeling they bring can pass with the wind or build up into a week-long isolation. Grief can wrap me up and drag me under. It has this hold on me.

We must understand as compassionate humans that triggers are everywhere for others. Try to put yourself in another's shoes and be aware of what some of those triggers may be. It's not possible to know them all, because even the aggrieved don't. But identifying obvious triggers and opening our minds up to what our family and friends may be feeling on a daily basis is truly being present with them in their grief. Awareness is key.

Examples of others being present in my grief:

- Friends give me a heads-up before announcing their pregnancy news on social media, which allows me time to process so I can celebrate with them.

- Our twins' names are said during family prayer.

- Family and friends allow me times of withdrawal: unanswered texts and calls, canceled plans, missed events.

- I'm allowed to have a moment of sadness on Mother's Day without questions.

And don't feel like you are walking on eggshells. Life is so complex, and grief is just another added layer. Everyone gets it wrong. I still do, to this day. I have put my foot in my mouth more than once. I understand it's a big responsibility to respond to those grieving, and it can feel like an incredible amount of pressure. Give yourself grace along the way. Just do your best to be kind and compassionate. We are all navigating this together.

"Do to others whatever you would have them do to you. This is the law and the prophets."

—MATTHEW 7:12

Chapter 13

The Club

There are so many realms of child loss. Infertility, miscarriage, stillbirth, infant loss. We can grieve the loss of hope, the loss of pregnancies, the loss of plans, the loss of future children. There is no black-and-white definition to describe the unraveling of our dreams.

After experiencing our own loss, I feel the doors opened. So. many. people shared their own stories of loss. My dearest and closest friends, family members, complete strangers. I would be bold enough to say that every single person I know has either experienced loss of their own or known someone who has.

When I was first going through our heartache—and still to this day—it was so comforting finding others I could truly relate to. I was already on their level and didn't have to catch them up to speed. I could authentically be myself without question. I have told so many others facing loss, "You now belong to a club no one ever wants to be invited to or be a member of. But you're surrounded by the most inspiring, courageous, and loving people. It is an honor to have you."

When I initially began thinking about my book and what I wanted to say, I imagined all the people in my life who have impacted me by sharing their stories. Every one of them gave me the courage to tell my own . . .

~~∽~~

Jill, Mother of Four – "Years of Infertility and Heartache"

Where do I even begin? It's hard to go back to a time in your life that was dark, lonely, financially exhausting, and empty.

My story starts when I was twenty-five years old. My husband, Travis, and I are high school sweethearts. We were just teenagers when we first met. After finally getting married after so many years together, we were so ready to start our family. I was able to get pregnant in the first six months of trying, but little did I know, I was about to experience my first real heartbreak. One day early in my pregnancy, I started spotting. I called the doctor in a panic and went in to have my first ultrasound. I was exactly eight weeks along. Nurses tried to convince me that it was normal to spot and not to worry too much—that it could be implant bleeding. When they put the ultrasound on, there was a heartbeat. Unfortunately, the heartbeat wasn't strong, and the baby wasn't measuring eight weeks along. My heart broke into a million pieces.

My next heartbreak was almost a copy and paste. It took another six months to get pregnant and I was exactly eight weeks along. I started cramping and spotting, called the doctor in another panic, only to find out the same news. I was living another nightmare. I had my second miscarriage. Of course, this was right before Christmas, which made it so hard to keep the happy "I'm fine" face on. In the first two years of our marriage, nothing had gone as planned. My dreams weren't unfolding how we anticipated. I had two babies in heaven, but no baby to hold.

After my second miscarriage, my doctor wanted to get a second opinion from a fertility specialist. That led to so many appointments and tests. Basically, none were covered by insurance. So, not only was I extremely stressed and my anxiety maxed out, but we were financially burning the candle at both ends. I ended up doing five unsuccessful IUIs (intrauterine inseminations), fertility treatments that involve directly inserting sperm into a woman's womb. Thank God for my husband, who was so understanding. But I knew deep down he felt so helpless and sad himself. After the fifth failed IUI, we had already spent the majority of our savings and my husband said it was time for us to think about other options.

Life was so painful at this point. Day to day, I had to move forward and continue taking that next step. But I was dying inside. I felt like people weren't relating to me or that my loss wasn't big enough to discuss. My friends were getting pregnant and I couldn't share in their excitement. I wanted to crawl in a hole and grieve, but life wasn't allowing it. I knew what the next step in our journey was, but could I handle the toll it was taking on me?

Next came IVF (in vitro fertilization): mature eggs are retrieved from ovaries and fertilized by sperm in a lab; then the fertilized egg, or embryo, is transferred to the uterus. The entire process pushes your mind and body to their limits. I went through all the shots, went to every appointment, and was so hopeful this was the answer to our prayers. I just wanted a healthy little nugget to hold and share all our love with. We had so much to give. I remember being so nervous for the egg retrieval process. They ended up getting eight eggs, which I was ecstatic about. This was it for us; it was our time.

After the incubation period, only two eggs made it through to become considered embryos "sufficient" enough to be implanted. Talk about having all your eggs in one basket. We went into the doctor's office to get the two embryos implanted. I wanted to vomit from the nerves. I remember after the implantation was complete, I felt mentally exhausted. I was crying. My doctor grabbed my hand, looked me straight in the eye, and said, "We will get you pregnant one way or another." I had this weird feeling that something wasn't good. I was uncontrollably shaking and crying the entire way home.

The two-week waiting period was excruciating. They tell you not to take a pregnancy test, but let's be real, I don't have that kind of willpower. I made it over a week without testing, and it showed that I was not pregnant. I tried reminding myself that's why they tell you not to test and that it could still happen. You literally read and look up every possible scenario on Google. Your brain wants to explode. Those two weeks went by, and it was time for the official results from my blood work. My first round of IVF was unsuccessful.

My world was falling apart. I felt like a failure as a woman. In my head, this was a home run to get us the baby we so desperately prayed for. IVF gets everyone pregnant. Well, lesson learned. I met with my doctor a few weeks later to find out no one knew what the official diagnosis was for why I was not staying pregnant. The doctor went into this whole explanation of what could be happening, but he didn't know for sure. He gave me a 10 percent chance of IVF working with my eggs and my husband's sperm. Yet another failure.

Why couldn't my woman parts just do what they were supposed to do? Now we had more decisions to make. Did we want to dish out another $20,000-plus? Could we even afford to? Well, *let me tell you, somehow God provides. If it's what you want, the money doesn't matter. I would spend every penny I had to get my family.*

One of the decisions we had to make was, do we want to use donor eggs, donor sperm, my eggs, my husband's sperm? The doctor said our best chance to get pregnant would be to use donor egg and donor sperm. We felt like this would be our last attempt at IVF. Mentally, I was wiped. The doctor knew my eggs were the issue, but couldn't tell me one way or the other if my husband's sperm had any part in it. After many discussions, we decided on donor eggs and my husband's sperm. It was so hard to give up that part of me, knowing my kids wouldn't look like me or have my freckles. It was almost another loss.

We decided to only tell our immediate family that our next attempt at IVF would not use my DNA. We had long, hard, tearful sit-down talks with each of our parents, but we wanted kids and were willing to do whatever it took. After more medications, and my selfless anonymous donor also doing medications, tests, and appointments, it was time for her egg retrieval. They got twelve eggs! My prayers were answered and I was so happy.

After the waiting process, I got the call and we had five viable embryos! Holy crap, was this really going to happen for us? Next was the implantation. We decided to implant two embryos, which would give us a better shot at this working but also a high chance at twins. We aren't millionaires so if we could get two in one round, we thought, Let's do it. We can sleep when we're dead.

The implantation day, I still had the vomit feeling and the shakes from my nerves. My guardian angels were with me that day. About two to three minutes after implanting the embryos, I was just lying there and I felt a weight come off of my chest;

a weight I had been carrying around for almost three years. I looked at my husband sitting next to my head, holding my hand, and I said, "I know this is weird, but I think I am pregnant this time." Something was different; I felt a sense of calmness and happiness. The entire ride home I didn't cry; I felt relief. I felt This was it. I think it worked.

Another two-week waiting period. Again, I told my husband I wouldn't take a pregnancy test this time, but I totally lied. I made it about one week, took a pregnancy test, and it was positive. The worst part was I couldn't tell my husband because I didn't want it to be a false positive (and I'd told him I wouldn't test). Our anniversary was the day before my official blood test to find out if I was pregnant. I surprised my husband with like five pregnancy tests, each one with a darker line than before. He was so happy. He said it was the best gift he could have gotten.

Since that positive pregnancy test, we have been blessed with two beautiful daughters. They are 100 percent biological, both using the same anonymous donor. We will never know her name or be able to meet her. But I thank God every day for her selfless and beautiful act that allowed our family to grow.

Except for my immediate family, no one has any idea we did donor eggs. I used to feel embarrassed. If I knew then what I know now, I wouldn't feel that way. I would be thankful. Do my kids look like me? Not really, but they look like my husband. I sometimes think I see me in them, which is weird, but man, do they have my personality—like I hear myself talking back to me half the time. They are my world. I regret nothing. God knew I needed both of my girls. They fill the pieces of my heart that at one time were shattered. Just know that if you are reading this and trying to start your own family, I pray for you. You can get through these dark times. Lean on your husband, family, friends, coworkers . . . They are your cheerleaders—heck, they are free therapists! Find your happy.

~~⟡~~

Jacklyn, Mother of Four - "You Should Be Here"

Her name is Isla. As much as I wish our story was different, this is us. And I love us to the fullest. Isla was the one to complete our family, yet my heart will forever have a gaping hole. I will never understand. I will never accept the outcome. But I am surviving. Some days surviving at an interval of heartbeat to heartbeat. But I am here, and I am here for Isla.

The truth is, Isla should be here too. And she is. It's just not how we had envisioned it. Not how we hoped it would be. But she is here. And to be honest, I do not want Isla to be anyone but who she is. So here we go; this is Isla.

Born silent at thirty-eight weeks and four days. Gentle hands, long eyelashes, and tiny toes. Every crevice, every wrinkle, and every fold on her petite body was examined. I knew that I had to remain present, for I would never get these moments back.

We learned of Isla's passing just three days before her scheduled birth when they were unable to detect her heartbeat. At that moment, I did not just lose Isla; I lost myself. So much was taken from me that day.

The ebb and flow of grief brings all the feels. From feeling absolutely everything, to feeling absolutely nothing. The numbness is real. Isla's death came out of left field for us. I could not even bring myself to believe this happened. And then to have to go through all the motions. Put simply, it was living a nightmare in real time.

To this day, I am not sure what hurts more—the shock of losing Isla or the wonder of what could have been. We never saw this coming. So unexpected. Gone too soon. I never realized the pain would last this long.

Sometimes it feels like forever since I last heard her name. So long since someone asked about her. Almost like she is a person of the past. But for me, I think about her every day. I want others to ask about her. To say her name. I want someone to bear witness to my pain. I want someone to acknowledge that grief belongs to the griever.

By sharing our stories, my hope is we can help our culture understand that conversations about grief are really conversations about love. This is Isla. She is my daughter. She is loved. She should be here.

Angela, Mother of Four – "Adoption Journey"

Adoption: complications, faith, beauty, loss, hope, love, and so much more. When my husband, daughter, and I started on our adoption journey we had no idea what was in store for us. So much emotion, so many dreams, so much uncertainty, and so much learning. Looking back, I wouldn't change a thing.

About one year after our daughter Claire arrived, Jeff and I were extremely excited to open our hearts to another child. The plan was four children, evenly spaced every two years. Turns out, God had a different plan for us.

After over a year of "trying" to get pregnant, we finally decided to seek medical help. What's going on? *We didn't get pregnant with Claire right away, but it certainly didn't take a year. So, we made our first appointments. He went to urology and I went to OB/GYN. We were both scared of the testing and results. After a few months of lifestyle modifications and more testing, we learned Claire was a miracle and getting pregnant would likely not happen again. The pain, the sadness, the anger, the embarrassment, the shame, and the jealousy started to set in. The hardest part for me is I am a generally happy, optimistic person. I was being consumed by one thing: my inability to have a second child. I wanted to know why.* Why me? What did I do to deserve this? *And the saddest part is I truly convinced myself that I had earned or deserved to go through the beast of infertility.*

After learning all that was ahead of us, we decided to move forward with IUI (intrauterine insemination). Jeff and I were not quitters. We always lived by the rule that we can get through anything. We could find a way to make things work. We wouldn't give up. *IUI is such a cold, lonely, sterile process to me. The man does a collection, and the fluid is spun down so only top swimmers move on. Then the sample is placed in the uterus via a tube. After that, you hope and pray for the next two weeks. Along with this procedure, it was recommended I take two medications, a pill and an injection. Talk about an emotional (and hormonal) roller coaster. I am already an emotional girl, but add on working a full-time job, being mom to Claire, being a wife, a friend, and a daughter. The ability to not cry continuously about the sadness that had taken over my head was exhausting.*

Unfortunately, the letdowns continued. After three rounds of IUI, we were still not pregnant. It seemed as though even IUI was not a viable option for us. Next up, in vitro fertilization or adoption. We both needed to take time for this to sink in. I felt like I kept bumping into signs, at church and in life, that were pulling my heart to adoption. I knew how I felt before, during, and after insemination procedures and I didn't know if I could take anymore—emotionally, physically, or mentally. But Jeff was not sure adoption was for him. His question was, Can I love another child like I love Claire? *I was convinced I could, but I couldn't love for both of us. We both had to be all in.*

We decided to move forward and at least meet with friends and acquaintances from our small town or work who had adopted a child. We met with three different people. God bless them for being open and honest about their experiences. They were confidential, caring, and understanding. God knew we needed them.

We decided to go to orientation at an agency. It was overwhelming, exciting, and scary at the same time. I remember hanging on every word, especially from one couple who came forward to share their experience. They were "chosen in one week." My heart and stomach fluttered! I had wanted to be a mother to another child for well over a year (and, really, my whole life) and now it could be "only a week away"! The roller-coaster ride was really going now. First, we needed to complete a home study. This was a series of meetings with a social worker asking about our childhoods, parenting philosophy, and physical home. This was stressful as well. The ups and downs continued, but finally the home study was complete and then we waited.

For me, the wait was so hard. Having so many emotions, longing for another child so badly. Feeling sad and selfish because another mother would bear and birth a baby that she would not parent. Being the sounding board for so many friends who were struggling with infertility only to watch them become pregnant. The feeling of hating going to Walmart and watching other parents yell at, grab, and belittle their children, when I was so desperate to have a child of my own. The struggle was real. Again, I am usually such a positive person, and the negativity was taking over my brain. That wasn't good for me, Jeff, or Claire. Having this attitude made me feel as though I was letting them down and it made me sad.

Waiting and calling, calling and waiting. This was my mode of operation. I would wait a few weeks and then call the agency. "Hi! This is Angela. Is there anything new?" Oh, if I could count how many times I made this call. The thing is, it was just something to do. Of course, the agency would call if anything was happening. But I just felt if I called, I was doing something active.

In hindsight my best advice would be to live in the moment. Instead of longing for something in the future or dwelling on what "might have been," just stay in the present. Look around and find reasons for gratitude each and every day. Daily gratitude is something I continue to this day. I lie in my bed each morning and think of three things to be grateful for and say a small prayer.

Fast-forward sixteen years.

Four beautiful children. Not evenly spaced every two years. A conspicuous family Jeff and I could not have created alone without the gift of adoption. This is the life that was meant for me and my family, and it is a treasure. It is my why. When I reflect on my journey it absolutely brings me to tears. At one time in my life, I felt as though I was being punished. Now I feel like I have been abundantly blessed. Every day is not easy, but every single day the six of us were meant to be together through the good, the bad, and, occasionally, the ugly.

If you've thought about adoption, continue to seek out those thoughts. Don't let fear take over; let hope, love, and promise take over. Trust God and your gut, and your life can be more beautiful than you ever imagined.

Nicole, Mother of Five Boys – "Choosing Life"

Our journey began when my boyfriend, Tory, and I found out we were expecting in August 2021. Our pregnancy began just as any other pregnancy had for myself. I was sick with morning sickness in the beginning, super tired, and oh so excited to meet our blessing.

At our twenty-week anatomy scan, we were on a telecom visit with a specialist in Rochester, to be addressing the uterine wall that I had developed from having four cesarean sections prior. Little did we know, at that moment they wouldn't be focused on my uterine wall, but on the finding that our baby had CDH (congenital diaphragmatic hernia). I remember just bursting into tears on that ultrasound bed looking over at Tory. Tory, being a first-time dad, wasn't quite sure what was going on.

The doctor kept telling us that we had two options, termination being the first one, which she repeated many times. The second was relocating to one of the seven states that offered a procedure in utero called FETO (fetoscopic endotracheal occlusion). FETO is a tiny balloon that would be inserted through our unborn baby's mouth while in the womb, in hopes of expanding his left lung, which was struggling to grow due to the hole in the diaphragm. That hole was allowing our son's bowel to be in his chest cavity instead of his stomach. After leaving our appointment, I looked directly at Tory, and at the same time we both stated, "We will never terminate!" We would give our beautiful baby boy to God and let Him decide the life he chose for Kai.

We prayed for one month straight after hearing our choices. We researched information on CDH, found groups for others who experienced CDH, and looked at locations and survival rates of the hospitals. One month of complete unknowns was the hardest.

In December, we met with a specialist in Rochester, Minnesota, to determine where to go next in our journey. Our specialist arranged for us to head to Texas Children's Hospital in Houston. On January 10, 2022, we drove nineteen hours in two days to be evaluated for the FETO procedure. After a day of scans, echocardiograms, and an MRI, the doctor called us at our hotel to tell us our baby wasn't as severe as Minnesota had stated and we didn't qualify for the procedure. We drove another nineteen hours home to Minnesota, the same day we'd left our appointments. The whole ride I cried. I didn't know what our baby boy would have to face and what his outcome would be.

From then on, we had to go to Rochester weekly to have scans and breathing exams. On February 8, 2022, I went to Mankato Hospital-Mayo to be monitored. I had been having contractions all morning and they weren't stopping. After getting to Mankato, they found I was dilating, and they couldn't risk delivering the baby at a place where a level-IV NICU wasn't available. They airlifted me to Rochester, where we stayed to be monitored, get steroid shots to strengthen Kai's lungs, and prepare him for early delivery. Thankfully they were able to stop the contractions, and we returned home three days later, with baby Kai still in the womb. We made it four more weeks until March 8, 2022, when Kai decided to make his arrival. My amniotic fluid was high, which is common with a CDH diagnosis.

The day Kai was born, he let out one tiny squeak in the operating room before he was whisked away next door and intubated. We got to spend the next five minutes gazing at his face, admiring how beautiful our blessing was. He then was transferred to the level-IV NICU at St. Mary's in Rochester, where he would fight for his life for the next unknown number of days. The first three days he was very critical, especially the third day when the doctors called us to meet with the ECMO (extracorporeal membrane oxygenation) team. The ECMO team places your baby on a lung-and-heart life support, giving him or her time to rest until he or she is able to have surgery. Thankfully, the following day his hypertension slowed down and he was able to stay on his oscillator vent. On March 14, Kai was able to stand the surgery needed to bring his bowel down to his stomach and close the hole in his diaphragm. He came out with no ECMO machine or chest tube, which is very unreal. The surgeon told us nine out of ten babies need a chest tube. Right then, I thanked God because he was the reason our miracle baby made it through so well.

On March 19, after eleven long days of waiting to hold our baby, Tory and I walked into Kai's room to find it so quiet. It was then that we realized he no longer had to be on the high vent. He was on a new vent, which allowed us to finally hold him. He was making such great progress; we were shocked! For the next few weeks, we just waited for him to no longer need the next medication and the next breathing apparatus. After each was discontinued, we were closer to all coming home!

On April 16, we were finally able to go home with no extra needs for breathing and eating. Kai was doing it all on his own. He overcame so many obstacles that we never doubted. We knew from the minute his diagnosis came in that he was guarded and guided by God. We had so many prayer warriors praying for us.

We had churches near and far spreading our needs. With the grace and faith of God, our miracle baby is thriving and living the life that we once thought he wouldn't. From the day we heard the word termination, *we knew we couldn't give up on our baby. We knew he needed us to give him every chance at life, and the outcome was in God's hands. We are forever thankful for God's abilities to heal the most unknown and difficult situations.*

Lisa, Labor and Delivery Nurse

As a labor and delivery nurse, the goal I have every day going to work is to help women (and families) welcome their child(ren) into this world in a safe manner. I have been involved in all kinds of situations throughout my career, but there is something about caring for families who experience preterm delivery or neonatal loss. When this unfortunate situation happens, it is essential to listen and to understand where your patient is at without judgment. This means I had to be vulnerable at times, as these situations are hard. You are not taught this in nursing school! It is essential that you inform and not provide false hope, but do so with compassion. This means making compassionate exceptions so the family has the opportunity to be with the preterm baby prior to transfer/separation or to room-in with the infant who was born still. Make that connection with your patient. You will make an impact—this moment in their life is monumental. They will never get this time back or have a chance to redo the situation.

I can name each baby I have been the delivery nurse for who was stillborn. There are features I remember that always stand out in my mind. *The crimson lips on one baby girl were so full just like her mom's. The full head of hair with a slight curl to the ends that a handsome boy had when he was born. The vision of a true knot in an umbilical cord that was tight and obvious with delivery. These images and names rest on my heart, even twenty-three years later. It is something that no one should have to experience. My heart aches for these women.*

I was Briana's nurse when she delivered Cohen and Calla. I was the nurse who checked her. I was the nurse who yelled "Run." When I came in to do her speculum exam early on that July morning, I remember thinking that she looked pretty uncomfortable to be that early in her pregnancy. Never did I expect to see a head of hair when I placed the speculum. I probably should not have yelled for the nurse to "run," as I probably created more anxiety for her and Luke, but I needed help and I was not leaving her side! Being on the cusp of viability is such a hard place. I knew she had the grit to hold those babies in until transport got there. Having Mayo present for delivery was the key in her delivery. They are the experts. We are trained to do resuscitations on preterm babies, but they do it every single day; we rarely do it, but we can do it. After their sweet babies left in the helicopter, I just remember the ache my heart had for Briana and Luke. Even as a nurse I was thinking, What in the heck just happened?!?

Fast-forward to Penelope. I saw Briana's name on the C-section schedule the day before she was supposed to come in. I remember having flashbacks of the July a couple of years prior. I wanted to be able to care for her, but did not know if she would be okay with that. I wondered if she associated me with the passing of Calla and Cohen. I called Briana and asked and she agreed wholeheartedly. I felt a connection, almost like something was telling me I needed to do this, for her and for me. The day came and beautiful Penelope was born. I am so blessed I could be a part of their story. I will never forget all of their babies.

Amalie, Mother of Four – "Born Still"

It never seems like words are good enough.

When I found out I was pregnant for the third time, I already had two boys. I knew this would be my last baby, and I desperately wanted a girl. My husband and I didn't tell anyone I was pregnant for four months; we just kept it to ourselves. This was different from my other pregnancies where I told everyone as soon as I knew. Since I so badly wanted a girl, we also decided we would not find out the sex of the baby until birth. I was at a friend's house one night, when her mom did the pencil trick to tell what the sex of my baby would be. You know the one—you tie a pencil around a string; if it swings one way it means a girl, and if it swings the other way, it's a boy. My friend's mom told me it showed three boys and then one girl. She said the timing was so close with the last one they could be twins or a year or two apart. I laughed and said she was crazy. I knew I was not having another baby after the third one, and I corrected her I was sure number three was a girl.

One night on my way home from work, I felt a pain in my stomach like someone was stabbing me. It hurt so much it brought instant tears to my eyes. I was worried about the baby. When I got home, I googled what it could have been. I was a little over twenty-two weeks, so the baby wasn't too big yet. Everything I read said it was fine. The baby probably just got caught up on the umbilical cord, but he or she would untangle in no time as he or she still had plenty of room to move around. I could still feel the baby move; it no longer hurt; so I thought everything was fine.

A couple months later at thirty weeks, I stopped feeling the baby move around as much. The kicks seemed to get [fainter] rather than harder like my previous pregnancies. I started getting worried and mentioned it to some of my friends. Everyone assured me the baby was just getting bigger and had less room to move around. Finally, I hadn't felt the baby kick in over two days. I went to the doctor's office, where they gave me an ultrasound. They had a hard time finding a heartbeat, and the nurse went to get another nurse to help. I knew something was wrong. Two nurses came back. They told me my baby no longer had a heartbeat and there was nothing they could do. I was in shock. My kids were there with me. I was trying to be strong. I didn't want them to see me crying. I called my husband at work and told him to come to the hospital. I was given the option to go home until my body went into natural labor or stay in the hospital to be induced and have the baby right away. I chose to have the baby right away.

My mom came and picked up my two boys. They were four and seven at the time. I delivered my third son on June 12, 2013. He was perfect! He had a full head of hair, and was two pounds, eight ounces, and thirteen inches long. I was surprised when I heard the baby was a boy because I was sure it had been a girl, and I had lost my chance at having a daughter. When I delivered the placenta there was a huge tear between it and the umbilical cord. It was obvious that the cord was hanging by a thread, and he had not been getting the nutrients he needed to grow strong and healthy. I immediately blamed myself as I remembered the day he pulled on his cord so hard. I was so mad I didn't go in to have it checked out that day. The nurses assured me that they wouldn't have seen the tear because it would have appeared like it was still attached on the ultrasound and his vitals would have been the same.

The nurse told me some people from Infants Remembered In Silence (IRIS) would come to talk with me. I had never heard of them before, and to be honest I didn't want to talk to anyone. They took pictures, provided a tiny little boy outfit, took moldings of his hands and feet, gave him a bath, and put a tiny diaper on him. He looked so handsome all cleaned up. I don't think I would have been able to clean him up like that by myself at the time. They were amazing, and I am so glad they were there for us.

The boy's name we had picked was Axton Allan. He didn't look like an Axton. I pictured an Axton as a wild boy with lots of energy. My baby boy lay there silent, looking like the sleeping cherub he was. We changed the name to Korbin Allan. It was a name I had liked earlier for one of his brothers, but my husband didn't like it at the time. This name seemed perfect for him.

We called my parents, and they brought my two sons to see their brother. My youngest son held him and sang to him. He was so happy to have a little brother, even if he was no longer alive. My oldest son was a little grossed out. He didn't want to hold the baby and stayed away. Before they left, the oldest boy did hold his brother and we were able to get a picture. We had a Baptism with a few family members. Then when everyone left, it was just my husband and our baby. We held him as long as we could and then it was time to say goodbye. We drove home crying, lay around crying for a day and a half, and then began to plan a funeral.

The day after my son was born, I found out that my friend's mom, the one who had done the pencil trick for me, had suddenly died in her home. I couldn't believe it. I couldn't get myself to go to her funeral because I knew I wouldn't be able to control my crying. Thankfully, since I hadn't learned the sex of our baby, we had hardly anything set up at home. We only had a few things to box up and put away. I looked up what Korbin meant for the first time and was happy to see "chosen for babies with dark hair." Korbin was my only child born with dark hair.

I returned to work two weeks later, and life went on as if nothing had happened. It was horrible. I cried by myself for months and months. I wanted another baby. My husband didn't. He didn't want to go through all that again. I begged and begged to give it a try. We tried for a year to have another baby and couldn't get pregnant. We were going on vacation, and I decided that when we returned, I would get back on birth control and we would stop trying to have another child. My boys were getting older, and I wasn't sure it was fair to have another so far apart in age. We got back from our vacation, and guess what? I was pregnant.

We were beyond thrilled, but also completely terrified. We had extra check-ups to make sure everything was moving in the right direction. When it was time to find out the sex of the baby, we decided we wanted to know. We went in for our appointment and they told us we were having a little girl. We were so happy. I began buying everything pink you could ever imagine. My daughter was born on March 3, 2015. She was perfect in every way, and we knew her brother in heaven had handpicked her for us.

I smiled to myself, realizing that I had in fact had three boys and one girl, with the last two being very close in age, just as my friend's mom had told me. It gave me comfort knowing she and my son were probably both saying "I told you so" to me while they looked down from heaven. My daughter is spoiled rotten by our whole family because she is the only girl. We told her how special she is and how her brother picked her from heaven. She talks about him all the time, and we celebrate his birthday every year at the cemetery. We participate in the Turkey Trot on Thanksgiving every year. It is a fundraiser for IRIS and a way to celebrate Korbin. We have a picture of his cute little feet hanging in the house next to his siblings' pictures.

The pain never goes away, but it does get better. We just find ways to include him in our lives as time goes by. After a while you realize you will never know the answer why it had to happen that way, but you learn to be thankful for the things you do have.

Laura, Mother of Seven – "God's Promise"

Up until our loss, my life seemed able to be planned out just as I pictured it. I got married to the love of my life, Scott, when we were young, just twenty-two and twenty-three years old. We planned to get pregnant after being married for one year and that happened just as planned. Our first daughter, Emmy, was born June of 2013. We were able to give her two brothers, Owen and Kade, each spaced out once again just as planned. We decided to try for one more baby to complete our family.

Up until then my pregnancies had been very easy and uneventful. My doctor always joked at how "normal" everything was with them. The appointments were quick and easy. In and out. We got pregnant with our fourth and what we planned to be last baby in August of 2019. We were so excited! We had never found out the gender of our babies prior to them being born and we decided to do the same this time around. Everything was going well with the pregnancy, and at our first ultrasound, baby was growing well. At my fifteen-week appointment, I was able to hear our baby's heartbeat. I swore I felt this baby's kicks around fourteen to fifteen weeks. The **best** feeling!

I never suspected anything was wrong until around eighteen weeks. I told my best friend I felt like my belly should be bigger for how far along I was. I wasn't feeling any movements, when I could have sworn I felt the baby move around that fourteen to fifteen-week mark. She calmed my fears and I, too, felt like everything was just fine, like it always was.

I had an appointment scheduled for November 27, 2019; I was nineteen weeks pregnant. That morning the weather was not great. We'd had a snowstorm the night before. I almost called to reschedule my appointment to the next week, so I could do the appointment and get the anatomy scan all at once. Looking back, I'm so glad I didn't do that. I told Scott he didn't need to come to the appointment, that we always wait so long to see the doctor and then the appointments only take five minutes. So, I went to the doctor by myself. That morning I had noticed just a small amount of spotting, but by the time I went to the doctor it was gone.

I told the doctor my concerns about not feeling the baby and about my belly size. She reassured me and said, "Let's listen to the heartbeat." She struggled to find a heartbeat, and I started to worry a little as she went to get the ultrasound machine. The minute she put the probe on my belly, my heart sank. The baby looked much smaller than I knew it should at almost halfway through my pregnancy and I couldn't see any flickering where I knew the heartbeat should be. The doctor confirmed my worst fear. The words no mother wants to hear: "I'm sorry, there's no heartbeat." I was so confused. What was happening? My doctor gave me a hug and told me she would send me to radiology to confirm with an ultrasound tech. I immediately called Scott and yelled into the phone, "There's no heartbeat!" He rushed to be by my side.

We had the ultrasound to confirm that our baby was no longer alive. The ultrasound tech asked if we wanted to know the gender, and we said "Yes." She confirmed our baby was a little girl. I lost it. I wanted to give our kids a sister so badly. I dreamed of having another little girl to complete our family. Two boys, two girls. I could hardly lay still enough for the tech to finish her pictures. My heart was breaking in two. We now had to make the decision to deliver our baby that night or wait until after the holiday weekend. The next day was Thanksgiving. The moment I found out she wasn't alive, I wanted her out. It seemed so barbaric to walk around with my small belly knowing there was no life growing inside of it. I wanted it to be over with. We got sent over to Labor & Delivery that day.

I had to give those dreadful calls and texts to family and friends, letting them know the news. The only other times I'd been in the hospital were the days my other children had been born. The sterile smell used to remind me of those happy days and now it reminded me of my worst nightmare. The next few hours were just a fog. It felt unreal. Why was I there? How could this be happening? Around midnight my contractions started getting intense and my water broke. It started to feel real, and I was crying. My nurse asked if I was okay and if I needed pain medication. I didn't know how to answer. I was in pain, but it was my heart just breaking. This was real, and I then realized the unbearable task ahead of me. I had to actually deliver my baby. My baby who would be so small and would not have a heartbeat.

The time came. It was the early morning hours of Thanksgiving Day. November 28, 2019. I pushed a few times, and my daughter came out in the palm of the doctor's hand. She was so tiny, but perfectly formed. She was placed on my chest, and we got to hold her and look at her perfect face. She had a little dimple chin just like her big sister. She had the tiniest hands and feet. They were able to get little hand and feet prints for us to take home. Our daughter was baptized, and we held her for hours. The time came to take her away. That was the last time I saw my baby. I remember feeling numb in the hospital. I was drained.

We then had to go home and tell our children. They were little at the time and didn't really understand. I could tell Emmy was sad to know her little sister wouldn't be coming home. We decided to have the kids help us give our daughter a name. We named her Lucy Elizabeth Miller. The next weeks were filled with tears and sadness as we tried to move on from that day.

Those days after, I didn't want to see anyone. I didn't want to hear "I'm sorry." I didn't want to make anyone feel uncomfortable not knowing what to say when, really, there was nothing to say. I lost my baby. The longing and grief were at times unbearable. It comes in waves. I felt like I could cry a lifetime of tears, and then the next minute I was so numb I couldn't cry even if I wanted to. Everyone else's life seemed to have forward momentum while I felt like I was standing still. I was so sad every day, but I carried on. It's amazing what the body can do with trauma. I stuffed it down and felt like after a month or so I was doing "good." I know now that I wasn't. The trauma and grief would rear their heads sooner or later.

We did genetic testing on Lucy and my placenta tissue. The results came back that there was no known reason why she passed away. I was grateful it wasn't a genetic defect that we could potentially pass on to other children, but we were left with wondering why. We then decided we were going to try for another baby as soon as we were able to. Our doctor gave us the go-ahead at the end of 2019. We were certain we would get pregnant right away, just like with the other four times. Little did I know it would take us eight months before we would see those pink lines on a positive pregnancy test. Dealing with grief from losing a baby was hard enough, and now add the longing for another baby. Each month passed and my heart would break over and over and over.

Around six months after we lost Lucy, I couldn't take it anymore. I felt like I was drowning in a sea of grief. I was so overwhelmed with everything. I didn't know who I was anymore. Lucy's due date came and went, and we had nothing to show for it. I started getting mad at God. Why would he take my baby from me and make me suffer now when trying to have another baby? Why?! Months had passed and I felt like everyone had forgotten what happened or thought that I should be "over it" by now. I could not stop thinking about Lucy and the baby we were trying for. It took up every moment of my thoughts. I finally had to get help. I reached out to my doctor to get medication and started therapy. This, along with leaning on God, is how I was able to get myself above water. I started to feel better, and happiness, joy, and other feelings started to coexist with my grief.

We did end up getting a positive pregnancy test in July 2020. I was so happy that the trying part was over. I took a small sigh of relief. That relief only lasted a few days when I realized it was a chemical pregnancy and my world crashed again. The next month, August 2020, came our rainbow. We saw those two pink lines on the test. We were finally pregnant again. The anxiety that comes with pregnancy after loss is another beast. The anticipation before every ultrasound was so overwhelming. We made it to May 6, 2021, and we welcomed our baby boy, Reed Holt Miller. He was so perfect and everything we dreamed of after our loss. He truly helped heal my soul.

Looking back on those months of waiting for our rainbow baby, as much as they hurt so bad, they were exactly what I needed to help me heal. They forced me to feel all the overwhelming feelings and got me to start medication and therapy. I think if I would have gotten pregnant right away, I would have suppressed those feelings even more. Hindsight is definitely 20/20, but God knows exactly what He is doing, and His timing is perfect. Do I think God took my daughter to "teach me a lesson," or to show that "everything happens for a reason"? No. Terrible things happen all the time. We can either fall into the dark hole of grief and trauma or we can lean into God, our family, and friends to help carry us when we are too weak to continue.

We talk about Lucy all the time. Our four-year-old, Kade, asks all the time, "When can we go to heaven to see Lucy?" We celebrate her birthday on November 28 with cupcakes and visiting her burial site, and on her due date, April 21, we light Chinese lanterns up to heaven. I now find myself smiling when I see something that reminds me of her, like a rainbow, a cardinal, or when people say her name. I think all the time about how she would have fit into our family. Would she pick on her brothers? Would she and her sister be best buds? But with God, I have the promise to see her again, and that brings me pea

Erinn, Mother of Four – "Preemie/NICU Mama"

I never knew what it meant to live your life as a witness. A testament. To walk by faith and not by sight.

None of us are really strangers to trauma or grief. We all have our own story.

There have been so many times that I have questioned God. Questioned why he would allow certain painful struggles to happen. It never occurred to me that I could be the witness to a beautiful faith, to a God who shows endless mercy in a world full of sinners. Miracles happen. The unexplained. The only real testament we will ever see on earth of a God who loves us endlessly.

Our miracle didn't come before grief and suffering. We'd lost before. A devastating miscarriage at ten weeks, a month before our first wedding anniversary. A failed D&C, followed by weeks of labor pains, never resulting in a healthy baby.

Labor and delivery is a miracle in itself. Our rainbow baby came a year later, perfect, without complications.

My husband wanted a soccer team of kids, and I felt I could make an attempt at maybe three players.

God is faithful. I'd get pregnant again by the time our daughter turned one.

Something seemed off with this pregnancy, almost from the start. At my seventeen-week appointment, the doctor was very concerned when she wasn't able to find the baby's heartbeat. I was rushed to an ultrasound room where they were able to see the baby and the heartbeat. Relief.

A month later, I would start having regular contractions. Each time I'd make a trip to Labor & Delivery and they'd give me medication to stop them. Week twenty-seven, Christmas Day. Unable to stop contractions and having already reacted to the medication, I was sent to Mayo. We met with a NICU doctor, and the grief set in that I would not make it to forty weeks. I was thankfully sent home, on moderated bed rest, with medication, and I had been given shots for the baby's lungs to help them develop a bit faster.

At thirty-five weeks I woke up to what I can only describe as a pop and a gush. My water broke. It was going to be fine. I was early, but I had those shots to help the baby's lungs.

Labor seemed normal. I had done this before; I could do it again. After little to no effort, I pushed our son out in one big push.

We heard one tiny shriek from our five-pound baby boy. The room fell silent. They didn't hand me my baby. The doctor immediately called a code and screamed for the pediatrician to be paged. The room was suddenly flooded with people. I could not look at my husband. If I did, I would break. I kept my eyes on our baby, or what I could see of him. Praying the rosary . . . Hail Mary after Hail Mary . . . begging for our son to stay.

Finally . . . after watching the doctor revive our tiny baby, she looked back and said, "We've got him, Mom."

They quickly gave us a glimpse of our intubated son before rushing him off for more observation and tests. The NICU team was on their way via helicopter to take our very sick baby to Children's Minnesota Hospital in Minneapolis.

His lungs were unfortunately still very underdeveloped for thirty-five weeks' gestation. We were able to have him baptized and given the anointing of the sick before he was taken by the NICU team. I was thankfully discharged less than twenty-four hours after his birth. We would rush to Children's, not knowing what we'd witness or do upon our arrival.

We named our son Liam, which means "strong-willed warrior." He was already living up to his name.

Liam would remain in the NICU for five more weeks. As a NICU parent, you never forget the sounds, smells, endless beeps, or even the lingo. I would live at the hospital learning everything there was to know about the ups and downs of a premature baby. Liam was on oxygen until two days prior to discharge. He was diagnosed with something called dysphasia, when a person cannot swallow properly. It can be common in premature babies and we were told it would resolve after a few weeks or months. Liam was on thickened formula feedings due to his condition. He would be sick with aspiration pneumonia several times over the next nine months until he was again admitted to Children's for an extended stay.

My heart would break endlessly for our son. I'd pray for healing and strength and for God to again grant us a miracle. He did. But not in the way I would've ever asked for. Liam needed a gastric feeding tube and extensive therapy three times a week in Minneapolis. After no longer being able to commit to working forty hours a week, I lost my job. Over the next few months, I was running on fumes. A sick child, a toddler, an extensive medication/doctor's appointment schedule. But I continued to pray and not lose the hope God gave me from Day 1. Liam would go through therapy and have his feeding tube removed two years later. Appointments dwindled. Our son, our miracle, he stayed.

The grief and trauma surrounding his birth and those days are still fresh, even after nine years. The faith . . . the small miracles . . . I hold onto every day. God is never far from your reach. He sits with you in the darkness, waiting for your plea.

Through everything we went through, leaning on my husband and our family was imperative. But also knowing this was a short moment in the long run, that these hard days would one day be a memory. I lived in the moment as best I could, gather-

ing my tribe of people to help get me through and knowing that this struggle wasn't forever.

One of the best NICU nurses we had actually encouraged that. She said something along the lines of, "Your time here might feel like forever, but it's so short in what will be a long life."

I really did cling to that over the next two years; all the tests and appointments. It felt endless and exhausting. But here we are nine years later and it's just a memory.

Except when he breaks his arm and we spend quality time in the emergency room.

～∾～

Sarah, Mother of Four – "Wings of Hope"

I found out I was pregnant with our third baby just after the new year. I'd been through this twice, so I knew I should have been excited and figuring out how and when to tell family and friends. From the very beginning, something in me was different. I didn't want to tell anyone. I didn't know why either.

At fourteen weeks, I started bleeding. I didn't have that at all with the first two. It wasn't much at first, but it didn't go away either. As the days went by, it got to be more. I went to the doctor for different tests and scans and everything seemed good. I didn't agree. They said some women bleed their whole pregnancy and have a healthy, full-term baby. Again, I didn't think I was one of those women. I had two major episodes of uncontrolled bleeding, which involved me passing out and 911 being called. I took an ambulance ride where I received a blood transfusion. But I was still hearing the same thing: "Everything seems fine." I ended up feeling just "icky" all the time. I wasn't put on bed rest but told to "take it easy" with two littles at home. Not the easiest thing to do! I spent every weekend in the hospital in May just because I felt like the bleeding was getting worse. I would get sent home and be told to "monitor it."

On the morning of May 20, I woke up and was having some pains with cramping. It was pretty mild and, I thought, just another part of the "icky" feeling I had been dealing with for weeks. The cramps started to get more intense and seemed rhythmic. I decided to time them and see what would happen. I never went into labor at home with the first two, so this was something new for me. They kept growing stronger and became about five minutes apart. I was at twenty-two weeks and six days. My doctor said if I was over twenty-three weeks that I should go to the Mayo Clinic in Rochester, as they have a NICU and that would be the best place to deliver.

We called my doctor and he said to go to Rochester. My mother-in-law took the kids and we were on our way. By that time, the contractions had gotten close to unbearable and not far apart at all. We only made it to the next town, which was fourteen miles away, and I knew we wouldn't make it any further. I was on the edge of the vehicle seat trying to get as comfortable as I could with the intense pain. I felt her head right there. I was scared to move. Without trying to freak out my husband, I said, "You need to go as fast as you can, and I sure hope the lights stay green because we aren't waiting at a red light!"

We got to the emergency room doors, and it felt like forever for a nurse to bring a wheelchair out. It was probably only a couple minutes in reality. Then a long trip to the Labor & Delivery wing—up an elevator, down a hallway, turn, more hallway, turn, and finally the door to L&D. The nurse took me right to a room and got me next to the bed and said, "Whenever the pain lets up, remove your pants and get on the bed." That wasn't happening, and I knew my baby was almost out. I just decided to go as fast as I could, so I stood up and whipped my pants down. I quickly turned, sat on the bed, lay over to my side, and she was out. No pushing or prepping. The nurses were all scrambling. I instantly felt this feeling of relief. A very strange feeling with the circumstances, but I didn't feel "icky" anymore. A few minutes went by and the nurse came over and said, "We are having trouble finding a heartbeat." I told her that it was okay; I knew there wouldn't be one and they didn't need to try any longer. The amount of calm I felt in that moment was very strange, but that feeling I had in the beginning that something wasn't right must have brought me to that sense of peace.

Stormy May: 13 ounces, 10.5 inches.

We spent the rest of the day with her and got to look at her perfect little body, her fuzzy little head, how much she would have looked like her big sister, and every little detail we could to help us remember her. We had a few close family members visit us and hold her before they took her. We had her funeral four days later.

Every year on her birthday we get together and write messages to her and send them up to heaven for her to read. We have cake or cupcakes or cookies. The kids usually help me make her birthday treat.

We received a story about water bugs and dragonflies that has really helped our kids understand death and why we can't see Stormy again here on earth. The dragonfly is now a major part of our life, and whenever we see one, it's her. The kids shout, "It's Stormy!" with excitement and then ask if she wanted to visit us. It always brings a smile to my face knowing she will never be forgotten or not talked about. The rays of the sun shining *through the clouds, the wind blowing through the chime I got on one of her birthdays—both are signs from Stormy, just letting us know she's here and watching us.*

Talking about her frequently has helped me cope. I struggle from time to time when my four-year-old asks questions that I can't answer for her to understand. But I usually cry a few silent tears and try to get through it. I don't want her to worry that her questions about her sister make me sad or that she shouldn't talk about her. She will understand better one day.

We also really enjoy doing fundraising walks or events for infant loss. It is so nice to have your family alongside you, as well as so many other parents and their families who know exactly what you have gone through.

My Stormy May will always be in my heart, but I know deep down God saved her from a lifetime of suffering and allowed her to be "born sleeping."

~⚬~

Addie, Mother of Four – "Endometriosis Miracles"

I was bent over at work in pain when I finally decided to go to urgent care. I honestly thought my appendix was rupturing as my insides were pierced with a pain so powerful it made me nauseous. Even at twenty-four years old I still made the call to my mom to go with me to the doctor and to reassure me that things were going to be fine.

Urgent care was packed and when I finally was taken back, I got a doctor who was slow and thorough. She wanted to check me for all kinds of things, including strep, which I thought was insane. As lots of negatives came back, she sent me down to the ultrasound tech as a last resort, and an hour later we had the results: two cysts on my ovaries that needed to be removed ASAP, so we scheduled surgery.

I remember leaving my husband Jakob and my mom in the waiting room as I went into surgery. Counting backwards from ten, nine, eight—and I was under. Waking up, I asked my husband and mom what my doctor had figured out. I thought I had braced myself for the outcome with all of the googling I had done and blogs I had read before surgery. But hearing out loud that I had stage IV endometriosis broke me. I started crying on the spot. I was newly married. I wanted babies so badly. I was built to be a mom, and I knew Jakob would be an amazing dad. I was so angry, so hurt, and so confused. Why was this part of my story? I doubted God. I doubted His plan, His purpose, His hand.

I had started a business a year before selling pillow covers online. It turned into a collection of faith apparel with God's Got This, the message that my Aunt Gina had preached before a nasty series of cancers won their battle. I wanted that message of faith to carry on, so God's Got This was printed on pillow covers, tanks, tees, crewnecks, and blankets. And as I was in the thick of needing to trust God—knowing He had this—I doubted.

Waking up from surgery I was told that the doctors had "burned" as much of the scar tissue and webbing as they could from the endometriosis on my ovaries and insides. In the waiting room Jakob, my mom, and his dad were told that IVF would be the smartest option if we wanted to conceive. No matter how much faith you have, it still hurts to know that your dream might not be your reality.

Three weeks later we had our first infertility appointment. We were told that a series of shots for six months would be the smartest move forward. These shots would put my body into menopause. *They would likely kill off a lot of the endometriosis still all over my insides and get my body ready for the next phase of trying to conceive. At $1,000 a shot that wouldn't be covered by insurance, this was a commitment, but we didn't hesitate. I was told to call the office as soon as my next menstrual cycle came and then we would start the shots.*

Three more weeks passed. I made the call to schedule the appointment. My back had cracked and other weird, usual symptoms of my monthly visitor were there. I jumped at the opportunity to get the shots going, being one step closer to a baby. God had bigger plans.

My period never showed up. I grabbed a pregnancy test before work one day, as my shot appointment was coming up soon. Sitting in the Target bathroom stall, I read it right away: positive. *Since I am a "doubting Thomas" I went and bought a couple more tests—the more expensive ones now. Yes indeed, those were positive too.*

I didn't want to get excited just yet, or even tell Jakob because he was also walking through this emotional journey with me. So "doubting Thomas" called the doctor's office and gave them my long saga of a story, and they had me come in for a blood test. An hour later my doctor called me, stunned: "You are pregnant, congratulations!"

God's Got This. He had written a plan all along. Had I trusted Him from the start, it wouldn't have been so emotionally taxing. I still don't know how or why He did it. And then did it twice. *Yes, I am blessed to be a momma to* two *baby boys now ages five and two. Why did He choose me—a sinner, guilty of everything and deserving of a nothing—why did He bless me? I am forever grateful. I pray over my boys every night: "Dear God,* thank you *for Brooks and Shep. Thank you for making me their momma. Keep your hedge of protection over them and help them to always love Jesus. Let them be amazing friends and witnesses for you. God bless them in more ways than I can imagine."*

I am forever grateful, and for that I will always tell this story of doubt, of faith, of redemption, of blessing, and of how big our God is. Learning to preach my own message that is now on thousands of T-shirts was humbling and still is. Whatever mountain you think you are facing, friends—God's Got This.

Melanie, Mother of Seven – "Unexplained Infertility and Loss"

There isn't a day that goes by that I don't think about you. I wonder what you would look like, what sports you would be in; I try to imagine you driving, amongst many other things, as you would both be sixteen years old. I go through many emotions some days, from being sad and angry at times, to blaming myself. And there are also days I smile and thank you both for the time I had with you; you made me a mother.

From the time we married, my husband and I both knew we wanted to start a family. We had no idea how long we would try to conceive and the journey we were about to begin.

We tried almost two years on our own to conceive and then met with our OB/GYN for advice and help. We went through a few cycles of Clomid [an estrogen modulator medication] before being sent to a reproductive endocrinologist. After many tests for my husband and me, our specialist came to the conclusion of "unexplained infertility." We went through a few more cycles of Clomid and then Clomid with intrauterine insemination without success. We tried another fertility drug with the IUI, and *after six cycles of that, we came to the discussion of in vitro fertilization. We had made it this far and wanted children, so we agreed we had to proceed. We met with our team and began the process. There was so much to do: medications, appointments, blood draws, and ultrasound appointments. We were all in.*

Our first cycle of in vitro didn't work. We went on to a second cycle of in vitro and had a very early miscarriage. We decided to try one last time. Our third cycle was successful. I remember being at work (I worked as a labor and delivery nurse) and going to have my blood drawn in the lab prior to the end of my shift. I was back on the floor when the lab called and said, "How's 432?" This was in reference to my quantitative HCG. Anything over 20 was a positive pregnancy test result. I cried tears of joy.

I was cautiously optimistic. We were pregnant again. My HCG numbers doubled, even tripled, very rapidly. I knew—I could feel it in my heart—I was having twins. We went to our ultrasound confirmation at six weeks and there you both were, two blinking hearts on the ultrasound screen. Hearing your heartbeats was the most beautiful, comforting sound. We left the appointment in tears, tears of pure joy and excitement. We couldn't wait and told our families within a few hours of finding out.

Fast-forward to twelve weeks. You both looked healthy, absolutely perfect. I was told we made it past a critical point; I could relax! I was so relieved—we made it to twelve weeks!

We were so busy preparing for your arrival, enjoying getting the nursery ready for our two bundles of joy, loving feeling your movements, seeing you at ultrasound appointments. We were now at twenty weeks!

I remember waking one morning, going about as usual. I had the day off and the painter was coming over. I was talking with the painter when I felt movement and then a little trickle. It was so small, I thought it was urine. After all, I was pregnant with twins and they were active. I had an OB appointment two days later and mentioned this to my nurse and OB. I told them I thought I was peeing my pants. I was assured this was just urine. My OB did an ultrasound in the office that day and assured me that both babies looked good and the fluid looked good. But this "trickle" continued.

Over the next few days, I was growing concerned. While at work, I mentioned again to my OB it was continuing. I even did a nitrazine test that was positive. But, again, I was told not to worry. I was "fine" per my OB. I had this gut feeling something was wrong but didn't want to keep asking and being made to feel stupid. Why didn't I keep asking? Would it have made a difference? Would things be completely different today? I struggle with that; the guilt is consuming at times. I find it hard to breathe, feeling such overwhelming grief and sadness.

I remember the night before you were born. I was working 7:00 p.m. to 7:00 a.m. on the L&D floor, feeling a bit more tired than usual. But I was almost twenty-one weeks at this point. I had an active labor patient who was dilated to nine centimeters. I was setting up the room, getting caught up on charting, as it was almost 5:00 a.m., and decided I should go to the bathroom before I got too busy. When I wiped, I saw pink-tinged mucus. I immediately told my coworkers. I then became the patient. My friends, my coworkers, helped me change, reassuring me things were all right, comforting a now very afraid, trembling woman.

They did an exam and sent a slide of fluid from my speculum exam to the lab, and I waited. I lay there hooked to the monitors listening to you, feeling how active you both were and praying everything would be all right. When the lab did call up to L&D, they told me the fern test was positive—that "trickle" was amniotic fluid. I had been leaking small amounts of amniotic fluid for almost a week. The nurses, my friends, then called my OB to come in.

When my OB came in, he sat down on the edge of the bed and asked, "What changed?" Nothing. Nothing had changed. I had asked so many times in office and out of office—nothing. They did a bedside exam and ultrasound. I was reassured you were both active, the fluid looked good. But you were too little to be born. I needed to be transferred to a higher level of care.

I cannot explain how strange it was to go from the caretaker nurse to a patient in a matter of minutes. I was then taking an ambulance ride with my close friends who just happened to be my coworkers. To be the patient. I was in a fog. I was terrified. I was in denial.

My husband met us at the hospital. The ride was only about forty-five miles, usually less than an hour long. But it seemed like hours had gone by. I just wanted to get there, to be "in their hands." They would help me, help my babies, and it would be okay. I was admitted to the floor and my husband joined me shortly after. The high-risk OB said he would start me on anti-biotics and bed rest. The "leak" at that time was small and could possibly reseal, and I didn't have a fever. Yet.

We were in the room going over every possible scenario, but were, again, cautiously optimistic.

Later that morning, I began to have severe nausea, vomiting, and chills, and I remember being so thirsty even though liquids wouldn't stay down. Within two hours, I had full-body goosebumps and was shaking uncontrollably. I couldn't stand. My temperature had gone to 106.7. I remember them saying I was being transferred to the ICU and the Arctic Sun cooling ma-

chine wasn't available, so they were ice-packing me around my head, armpits, and groin.

I was met in the ICU by many physicians and nurses. I remember certain things, but not all. I was in septic shock from the prolonged rupture of membranes and infection and my organs were shutting down. They wouldn't let my family see me and my husband could only be in there at certain times. I remember yelling, arguing, going on in the room and multiple IV and PICC line attempts. I remember medications being given to save my life that I had only used before on critical patients to support blood pressure, as mine had bottomed out. My heart rate was over 180. But all that I thought about was our babies. I knew things weren't going well. I didn't want to lose them. I loved them. I still love them so much. I wanted them here on earth with us, to watch them grow, see all their "firsts." To hold and touch them, hug them, and kiss them.

Our daughter, Finley Rae, was born first. She was a fighter. She was so beautiful. She had dark features, the hair and all. She looked a lot like me. Chase Douglas was second to be born. He looked like his daddy. His tiny body was so perfect, his lashes, his fine light hair. So beautiful and perfect. He was trying so hard to breathe, but his body was too fragile and it was too early. I prayed to God. I prayed so hard.

We lost our babies. We had them baptized in the ICU. We had IRIS at our bedside to give their first baths, to dress them, and they fought for us. They truly fought for us, as did a very special couple of nurses who drove up and stayed in the ICU waiting room. I can never thank them enough. I was so fortunate to have known and worked alongside IRIS. They offer support, resources, and so much more. I never thought we would be the ones needing them. But there we were. I felt like it wasn't *real. I wished, at the time, I would have died also. I know that is horrible to say, but I truly felt such darkness and sadness. I felt as though I was in a deep, dark hole and would never see light again. Even with all the love and support of my husband, family, and friends, I was numb. My heart ached.*

We spent a few days in the hospital and were able to have Finley and Chase in our room with us for short periods at a time. Even though I didn't want them away from me at all. The hospital said they really "didn't do that" when I asked multiple times to have them with me, to hold them, and tell them how sorry I was. I felt responsible and to blame. At times I still feel that way. I can't explain, but it has forever changed me.

We planned their funeral, in between mourning and break-downs and having to go pump because my breasts were so engorged they hurt. I tried to donate breast milk, but the option wasn't available to us at that time. We never thought we would be where we were at that time in our lives, or ever for that matter.

We had a Native American healer speak and bless our children at the cemetery. He spoke of the rain and sleet, as it was so cold that day in March. He said the babies were telling us not to mourn their deaths, not to cry, that they were no longer suffering and at peace. From that day forward, every time we go to the cemetery, it is cold, overcast, snowing, or raining. I believe it's them telling me not to cry, that they are safe in Jesus's arms. They are being loved and cared for by family in heaven. My grandmother lives for her grandchildren. I envision her rocking them and loving them until we meet again.

The next months were a blur. I tried to go back to work as a labor and delivery nurse. I couldn't. I would have such anxiety that I would vomit and break down in the parking lot. Even stepping foot into the hospital made me cry. It brought back so many memories, it hurt. It killed me to see anyone pregnant or having babies.

My marriage was stressed; my husband chose to be away from me. Who could blame him? I was a mess. I didn't want to leave the house or talk to anyone and kept replaying events. I blamed myself for not "making" my physician listen to me. He didn't stop and listen; he just blew me off. I knew something wasn't right. Why didn't I fight harder? What did I do wrong to deserve this? I felt I had let my babies down and they weren't here because of me.

To this day, I still find myself replaying events in my mind at times, wondering how things would be different. I feel torn and guilty also for thinking that way, but it's the truth.

Finley and Chase made me a mother. They gave me such a beautiful gift to be their mom. I will always be their mom. I think of them, pray to them, and speak their names often. I learned to be more compassionate as a nurse, especially for those suffering miscarriage, stillbirth, or any kind of loss. They made me a better person. I am stronger and grateful for all they have given me. I would give anything to have them here with me. It gives me comfort to believe they were meant for more, and they are at peace and aren't hurting. I know how many medical challenges we would have faced had they survived so premature. I didn't want to lose them and never had imagined that as part of my life plan. But here I am, lying in bed while we are on a family fishing vacation in Canada, telling my story with tears rolling down my face. I still feel so many emotions, but most of all love for my babies, Finley and Chase. And also how blessed we are to have our living children here with us.

We talk about Finley and Chase; we visit them; we pray every night. Our children know they have a big sister and brother in heaven looking out for them and protecting them. When we think about them, we believe Finley is a silly girl, always playing jokes on us and keeping our spirits up. Every balloon release, Finley's balloon gets stuck. Her candle always goes out, her name is left out at services, and ornaments are spelled wrong. We know it is her. She was our fighter. Her name means "bittersweet."

We imagine Chase just watching his sister, calm and quiet. Chase was our warrior. I can feel his gentleness. Peace fills my heart and mind thinking about my spunky little girl and mellow little boy. Gosh, I miss them.

Our loving children, Darby (fifteen), Malia (thirteen), Baron (ten), Corbin (eight) and Crosby (six), will always know how loved they are and how blessed we are to have Finley and Chase in our family. Even though they aren't physically here, we feel their presence. They gave us what we have today. We have overcome so many obstacles; our marriage survived after almost collapsing so many times. We are stronger now than we have ever been. Not a day goes by I don't think of my first children. After all, they made me a mom. I still find myself sad at times, looking for answers, wondering why this happened. But I look into the eyes of my children, and they give me strength, love, and courage. If we hadn't experienced such heartache and loss, where would we be today? Things would be so much different.

Finley Rae and Chase Douglas taught me so much and brought me so much in life. God chose me to be their mom. After all the darkness, I feel there is light. A light I never thought I would see again. That deep love our family has for our babies in heaven, words cannot describe.

We just went by an eagles' nest and saw two eagles sitting together. My ten-year-old said, "It's Finley and Chase looking over us, telling us it's okay and they love us." My heart.

~~~

Ashley, Mother of Three – "Mighty Myles"

I had walked out of that unit hundreds of times, maybe even thousands of times. I'd ridden the elevator to the underground parking ramp and walked to my car many nights, hoping to reach the Ronald McDonald House in time to get a few hours of sleep before heading back to the hospital before sunrise. Each time I walked out and drove my car away from the hospital, I could feel my heart sink so far into my stomach that it felt like there was a heaping hole in my chest. It caused me physical pain and emotional turmoil to leave my baby at the hospital alone. When Myles was in the NICU, I wasn't allowed to spend the night with him. When he moved to the pediatric intensive care unit (PICU), I was allowed to stay, but encouraged by the incredible and dedicated nursing staff to leave and sleep. At that point, Myles was being given heavy sedation medication to help him sleep through the night, and the nurses knew that a little sleep was good for both of us.

On May 6, 2020, I carried Myles from that underground parking ramp, through the hallways of St. Mary's and up to the PICU, for the very last time. I remember that he felt heavy. He was three years old and had so many medical devices connected to him. But it was the last time I was going to be able to carry him anywhere, and I wasn't going to miss that opportunity for anything. We reached the front entrance of the hospital and there was a woman standing at the door, asking me to set Myles in his chair so that she could make sure we were all following COVID-19 precautions. With tears in my eyes and my heart on the floor, I refused. She didn't ask me twice.

Myles, Mike, and I made our way to the PICU on the third floor. The staff buzzed us in and we walked to the back of the unit. Everyone knew why we were there. Everyone knew that our son was going to die that day. When we reached the nurses, they were crying. At this point, that's all any of us could do. The first nurse to hug me removed her nursing smock, revealing that she was wearing her Mighty Myles T-shirt. All of the nurses behind her did the same. If there had been any pieces of my heart to pick up off the floor prior to that moment, that was no longer the case. My entire heart was now melted into a puddle.

After a few minutes of heavy tears and hugs, the nurses showed us to our room . . . his room. The room he had spent months in after receiving his tracheostomy. He would return multiple times and spend months sleeping over with his favorite nurses. It was our "home away from home." The sweet nurses had covered the room in superheroes (Myles's trademark) and had wings behind every one of them. Again . . . I was speechless and broken.

The next ten to twelve hours were emotional, devastating, and completely unbearable for [my husband] Mike and me. We sat with Myles and held him tightly as the medical staff helped him slip into a deep sleep, and eventually removed all of the medical devices that had been attached to him for his entire life. We played his favorite songs, read him his favorite books, read letters others had written to him, and just loved him in the fiercest way that we knew how. Around 11:00 p.m., Myles took his last breath. I held him as he slipped from being earthside in my arms, to floating straight into heaven. Mike and I continued to hold him while the hospital made arrangements and checked in on us.

At about 2:00 a.m., we walked out the doors of that unit for the last time. My heart didn't sink this time. It couldn't have. It wasn't even inside my body. My heart was still in the room of the PICU where my son spent his last day with me. I always assumed that I knew how I would feel walking out for the last time. I thought I would feel angry, sad, and uncontrollably broken. I thought for sure that someone would have to hold me and drag me off that unit. But that isn't what happened. That isn't how I felt. I was numb, just like I had been for days. My feet were moving, but I wasn't sure how. My face was wrinkled from the immeasurable number of tears that had fallen on it for the past week. My body was weak with disbelief and pure devastation. I was in denial, thinking this couldn't possibly be the end of this life we had grown to understand and call routine. I couldn't possibly be leaving my son at the hospital alone indefinitely. I couldn't be walking away from a staff that had become family to us for the very last time. All of those realities would hit me soon, but walking out those doors didn't feel like a real experience as it was happening. This couldn't be it.

When we entered the parking garage for the last time, we were met by our sisters and finally able to just cry. We cried loudly with intense pain. This was it. This place that we called home for three years had just turned into a completely different place in my mind. The doors didn't look the same. The faces that met mine outside didn't hold all of the hope and inspiration that they had the day before. Myles had died and what was happening was very real.

And still, even though the worst day of our lives took place within those walls, St. Mary's will always be a miraculous and untouchable place of gratitude and love for me. Even though our story, Myles's story, was written with an outcome that we *wouldn't have chosen, we were given an incredible amount of love and support from the NICU and PICU staff at Mayo Clinic. God had a plan for Myles. He reached an overwhelming number of people in his short life. He continues to inspire and make life brighter from heaven. He truly was a miracle.*

Leslie, NICU Nurse of Eighteen Years

The NICU is a world all its own. Unless you have a baby there and have been through it yourself, you can't understand the emotional roller coaster that these families go through. I have been a NICU nurse for seventeen years. I have laughed, cried, experienced miracles and loss. I feel honored every day to care for preemie babies and their families. Getting to meet tiny humans on their birthdays and watching them grow and develop, with the goal of sending them safely home, is the reason I am a nurse. But I definitely won't claim to know the whirlwind of emotions and stressors that NICU families go through during and after their journeys.

Preemie babies are strong and fragile at the same time. It is hard to imagine that a diaper change, a small change in position, or even a loving touch from their mom and dad can decrease their stability. Trying to promote bonding between parents and their infant, when the infant is born so early, can be very challenging. Many times, these tiny babies don't tolerate any touch, and that can be very scary and sad for parents who just want to bond with their baby. There are many instances where parents in the NICU experience loss of control and normalcy. I ask parents how they want their day to go. I can't imagine how it must feel to a parent when they have to ask if they can touch or hold their own baby.

Preemies are fighters, and although they can be sensitive and fragile, sometimes all they need is their mom's or dad's voice speaking softly into the port hole of their incubator to stabilize their vital signs. One of the highlights of my day is assisting a mom or dad laying their hands on their tiny baby or holding them for the first time and seeing the joy and nervousness in their faces.

Through all the breathing tubes, CPAP prongs, feeding tubes, central lines, and dings and dongs on the monitor, preemies test the strength of their families and providers. I remember while taking a report from the previous nurse, I asked about how the family was handling the news of a non-reassuring prognosis for their daughter. She responded, "She was so critical all day. I was so busy trying to meet her needs that I didn't have much time to talk to family." It can be overwhelming for family and staff. We both want to do what is best for their baby. As a nurse, I feel the responsibility of doing everything right, paying attention to every little detail, and keeping all the doctors updated on changes. While all the medical tasks are covered, I want to make sure the parents have trust in me and that their needs are met by assuring they have as much quality time with their babies as possible. Parents, I imagine, feel the stressor of their son/daughter being so critical and the care of that child being out of their hands. All they can do is pray and hope that he/she will become stable.

As babies get stronger, it gets easier to have bonding moments and parents learn what their little one likes and dislikes. I always say babies may not be able to talk, but they can sure tell us what they want. In the beginning, preemies tell us what they like by their vital signs changing. But, as they become more stable, they are expressive in their movements and actions. I love watching these tiny babies grow and develop personalities. Parents grow too, and I am always amazed by their resiliency and strength as they juggle life and their new normal in the NICU.

One day is smooth, the next is rocky. Some little ones have more obstacles to overcome, and as hard as they fight, they cannot overcome all of these complications. Some babies make their own decisions to end the fight, but others have parents who lovingly make the brave and selfless decision to take them off support, hold them in their arms, and tell them goodbye.

A family that holds a huge place in my heart is the Hoisingtons. I got to meet Cohen and Calla on July 2, 2013. They were born at twenty-two weeks' gestation, two of the youngest babies in our NICU. I had the privilege of caring for Cohen on his first day of life. I briefly got to meet Luke on July 3, as he visited their newborns. I remember how loving, excited, and nervous he was. Sadly, Cohen passed away on July 4. I was blessed to become one of Calla's primary nurses. I got to take care of her every day I worked and built a relationship with Briana and Luke. Calla was fragile and very critically ill. She was sensitive to everything, but I remember Briana and Luke placing their hands on her and talking to her, which would stabilize her vital signs when she was having a bad day. They would sit at her bedside day in and day out for hours. We had many conversations. I loved how Briana could express what they were going through as a family. From these conversations, I learned so much about being a caring nurse for not only the tiny babies in the NICU, but also the whole family.

I remember getting the call at home that Briana and Luke had gotten bad news regarding Calla's prognosis. I came in and got to kneel down beside Briana as she held Calla for the first time. We visited about the news they were given and the impossible decisions that were being asked of them. I told her how lucky her children were to have such wonderful and caring parents and how blessed I felt that I got meet and care for her son and daughter. Calla fought hard, but when she was twenty days old, she had too many complications and life support was removed.

After their journey in the NICU ended, Briana and I kept in touch. I loved receiving her emails, and she helped me understand what families go through after their NICU experience. In time, she was able to come back to the NICU to visit. She expressed how hard it was, but also how it helped her heal. She and her mother brought in small bereavement blankets for other babies and families going through the same experience that they had gone through. Some families and events shape you as a nurse. As heartbreaking as it was to experience this loving family losing their beautiful babies, it made me realize that this is my calling and the only thing I imagine myself doing.

No matter how many hours, days, weeks, or months a baby spends in the NICU, I bond with them and their families. In some circumstances, I am one of the few people blessed to meet these little ones. In other situations, the baby has been with us for months. In times of grief, we all want to say and do the right things. Everyone grieves differently. Sometimes I sit and listen, and other times I cry with parents and talk about how much their baby is loved. I try to speak from the heart, and although I don't always have the right things to say or do, I hope that my presence and support eases their pain in some way.

Stephanie, Mother of Four – "Forever Loved"

I was nineteen years old and had just escaped an extremely toxic relationship. I couldn't believe it when I saw those two little pink lines. I went back to the abusive relationship hoping that a baby would turn him into my happy ever after. Shocker—it didn't.

My sweet JT was born August 3, 2005. I immediately loved him so much and was so ready to be his mama, despite not being anywhere near ready by most people's standards. Through becoming his mama, having to fiercely protect us from his dad, working to financially support the two of us while putting myself through school, I grew up really fast. I learned quickly and on my feet.

When JT was two years old, after a healthy birth and childhood thus far, he suddenly felt really hot; then he turned blue, lifeless, and his eyes rolled back in his head. My best friend called 911 while my dad did CPR. I thought I was definitely losing my baby. After a few long minutes, he came out of it and the EMT told me it was a seizure. Once we got to the hospital, the diagnosis of febrile seizure was given and I was told it would probably never happen again.

But it did. And then it happened without fever. He was diagnosed with epilepsy shortly before his third birthday. I had no idea how it was going to consume our lives for the next nearly eight years. Throughout those years, his seizures worsened, his development delayed, no medication worked, and they all had devastating side effects. JT had just about every type of seizure there was and days with hundreds of seizures. He had ESES (electrical status epilepticus during sleep), so while sleeping, he had constant seizure activity in his brain. We spent countless days and nights in the hospital. There were surgeries, infusions, and so *many medications. In between all of this, I tried really hard to make sure JT could be a "normal" kid. He loved baseball, dogs, going to theme parks, roller coasters, riding his bike, and playing* Madden. *Seizures accompanied most activities, but he didn't let them stop him. He was a bright spirit and a wise soul, who had a deep love and understanding of spiritual things beyond anything he learned here on earth.*

JT and I really grew up together. Our bond was intense. I was his mama bear, and our love was fierce. I had fulfilled my dream of becoming a registered nurse. After eight years of failed treatments and no further options, I was desperate to ease the suffering my son was going through. At that point, the seizures were so bad he had a home health nurse and a hospital homebound teacher. My heart was breaking watching him deteriorate.

I heard so much about CBD oil helping kids with seizures. I knew I had to give it a chance. But the amendment didn't pass [as expected] in May 2015 to legalize medical marijuana in Florida. JT had a hospital stay that resulted in further medical trauma and his neurologist telling me they would retry medications that had already failed for him. I decided right then what I had to do, and two weeks later, we left. Just me and JT. I got a job as a travel nurse and we headed across the country to Colorado [where medical marijuana was legal]. It was so scary and overwhelming, but I was so full of hope and excitement.

It was JT's first and last flight.

Seemingly miraculously, the CBD oil started helping. JT went two weeks seizure free, which hadn't happened in eight years. I thought this was the end to the struggle and his life was going to be normal. I really started to let my guard down.

JT went to sleep on September 17, 2015, after a great day of swinging at the park, eating peanut butter and jellies, and no seizures, and he never woke up. *The day my life changed forever.*

My son died of SUDEP (sudden unexplained death in epilepsy patients) one month after his tenth birthday. There were eight years of awful seizures and medication side effects. I often wonder what life would have been like if CBD were an option for him earlier. I wonder many things about his medical care. There are a lot of unanswered questions in epilepsy. I found that out the hard way a few years into our journey.

In the years since my son's death, I have felt him so strongly pushing me along in this life. He led me to find a deep love just months after his death. A man who, from the very beginning of my CBD experience, was just there to help my son. He is a better person than I could ever imagine. He gave me hope when I had none and has loved me so fiercely through my immense pain.

When I lost my JT, my whole world was him. I never thought I was going to survive. I would binge-watch Intervention, so sure something like that was going to be my end story. I would drive around sobbing, hoping a semi-truck would hit me and end the pain. But with support, a lot of love, and therapy, I placed the broken pieces back together a little at a time.

JT now has two little brothers here on earth. Leo and Maclan bring me more joy and happiness than I ever thought possible. This year, JT gained a baby sister, Cambry Aspen, in heaven with him. I lost her at fifteen weeks of pregnancy and unwillingly dove deeper down in my grief journey.

I never thought I could survive all the pain I have endured, yet here I am somehow still surviving, and dare I say, even thriving. The pain is still as deep as it was that nightmarish day seven years ago when I was pulled out of a work training course and told in a room of strangers, "JT died." I have had to learn to live with this pain that buckled me. The pain I thought was going to *end me is now incorporated into every aspect of my everyday life. My happy is tinged with sad; each moment is accompanied by bitter. Everything is different. At times I struggle and at times I seem to soar. I know the precious experience that this life is. I love harder. My life crumbled in seconds with two words, so now I try my damnedest to be as unapologetically authentic as I can, however messy or beautiful that is. Ultimately, though, what a beautiful gift it was to be that special boy's mama for ten years here on earth and forever in spirit. I am not sure if I learned more in his ten years of life or in the seven years since his death. I have no doubt he is going to keep enlightening me the rest of my days. I raised him, but really, he raised me.*

Hillary, Mother of Four – "Forever Remembered"

I thought it was strange that at thirty-eight weeks pregnant, my belly was not wiggling as I ate a Blizzard from Dairy Queen. It was a Saturday afternoon and I was coming home with my best friend from another friend's baby shower. Throughout the weekend, I was feeling my baby move every once in a while and reassured myself that I would be fine until Monday, when I had a doctor's appointment.

On Monday morning my husband, Ben, and I decided that if we were having a girl, we would name her Hattie. We already had a boy's name, Sawyer, picked out. I told him that he did not need to come to this doctor's appointment because I was confident everything was fine and he could stay home with our two-year-old son, Charlie. I also told him after the appointment, I was going to get diapers and a baby girl outfit just in case we had a girl.

When I got to the appointment, I told the nurse my concerns so the doctor came in right away. She calmly took me to the ultrasound room—at the clinic I went to, it was normal to have an ultrasound at every visit, so this did not seem worrying. Usually, the ultrasound room is filled with heartbeats, growth statistics, and sighs of relief. This time it was silent until Dr. Brien said, "I can't find a heartbeat." I was shocked! I remember shouting, "This happens this late in the game, Dr. Brien?" She comforted me and got the nurse to be with me while another doctor confirmed what she did not hear. I called Ben and he rushed to my side. I don't remember waiting for Ben or getting home; I think I was still in shock and disbelief. We had to decide if we were going to deliver our baby that same night or the next day. This was the one and only easy decision I would make for a while! I needed time to get my head wrapped around everything that was happening. What I really wanted was as much time with my baby as I could have. I needed one more night with her or him.

That night as Ben and I mourned, we started one of many brutally honest conversations we would have. If we had a girl, should we still name her Hattie? It was our first pick, but we also really liked the name Reese. Would we be wasting our favorite name? Were we terrible people for even thinking this? How were we supposed to do this? How were we going to survive this?

This was a whole new world to us because we did not know anyone who'd had a stillborn baby. We knew of people who had had miscarriages, but really didn't have a clue as to what they went through.

As we walked into the hospital to check in, the attendant immediately knew by looking at my red, swollen eyes that something was wrong with this woman who was supposed to be happily delivering a baby. The attendant did not skip a beat and *graciously directed us. At that point, I knew that there was some kind of note telling him about our situation when he checked his list. I was so relieved that I did not have to explain this to a complete stranger. As we continued to the delivery ward, we walked through the children's section of the hospital and the tears streamed down my face. The thought that we were walking into this hospital with our baby and we would be walking out with nothing was devastating.*

Our nurse and doctor were heaven-sent to be the perfect match for us and our situation. They catered to my every need, made sure I was comfortable every second of the day, and became our dear friends.

On Tuesday, March 19, 2013, at 5:30 p.m., I delivered a baby girl named Hattie Leigh. She had lots of dark hair like her dad! Her big brother, Charlie, has blond hair like his mom and dark eyes like his dad. So, I believe that Hattie had green eyes like her mom!

We were able to hold Hattie as long as we wanted and take pictures. Ben showed her the beautiful sunset out our hospital room window. Our grieving parents came into the room, and I excitedly announced that we had a baby girl and then immediately remembered she wasn't coming home with us. Our parents had mixed feelings about holding Hattie, which I didn't understand at the time. Now I recognize that they were grieving the loss of their only granddaughter and they were in agony for their own children who were struggling to navigate the worst experience of their lives.

Once we were home, we did not know what to do with ourselves. It was March, so college basketball was on in full force as we zoned out, trying to figure out our new normal. I remember the pain as my milk came in and the sadness as I thought, this is not what I am supposed to be doing right now. In a daze, we planned a funeral only because the funeral director was a pro at her job. The question the funeral director could not help us with was, what will she wear? We had no baby girl clothes. We had to go to the mall and shop for a baby outfit. It was Easter time with dresses everywhere. I put so much pressure on myself that this would be the one and only outfit I would ever get to buy Hattie. It had to be perfect. Again, my eyes were red and swollen and now my belly was swollen with no baby inside of it or in a stroller that I was pushing. The salesperson read my body language quickly and guided us to the perfect outfit. We kept the funeral to close family and our best friends. To our surprise, our nurse and doctor made the forty-minute drive to attend Hattie's funeral.

Fast-forward ten years, and we have had two more children after Hattie, Isaac and Reese. We celebrate Hattie's birthday every year, and we finally have found a way to make her birthday a fun family occasion instead of mourning her all day. The number of life lessons Hattie has taught me are numerous and priceless.

Chapter 14

Amongst the Ashes

Don't let what has happened, where you are, or where you are going determine God's love. Let it show you how to define God's love.

Everyone fails, makes mistakes, or takes a wrong path. Heartache, pain, anger, and frustration are part of our lives. Bad things happen to good people. We can't run away from the hurt.

I was twenty-seven years old when we buried our twins. I had just become a wife. Then a mother. *This* was never supposed to happen to me. I couldn't help it—I was mad. I was mad at God. *How could you? How dare you take my babies from me? What did I do wrong? What am I being punished for? How can I go on when my children are gone? Why didn't you stop this from happening?*

I may never know why God allowed our children to have such short lives on earth. But, no matter what, I want their lives and their deaths to have meaning.

Cohen and Calla are in the arms of our Heavenly Father. But because of those "circumstances":

- My children are free of pain and suffering, in a place of complete contentment, surrounded by incomprehensible beauty and joy.

- Penelope and Maclen are ours.
- I found out I could be stronger and braver than I ever thought possible.
- My love for my husband multiplied and our marriage only deepened with trust, hope, and faith. We leaned into each other and found our way hand in hand.
- I found God.

I don't think these are the *reasons* we lost our babies. This didn't happen so I could learn a lesson. But I choose to find meaning in my pain. I choose to find meaning in my *circumstances*. Though our circumstances will continuously change, we as humans will grow and evolve; we will triumph and fail. Our God will remain. He will not falter. His love is unending and so perfect.

Although I cannot look you in the eyes as I tell you this, and I cannot hold your hand for you to feel my sincerity, I deeply pray you can feel my utmost and heartfelt love coming from a genuine place of hope in my wishes for you:

- I wish you could see yourself through the eyes of those who love you. Full of complete love, adoration, and joy. God made us to love ourselves and others as He loves us.

- I wish you would take the time to just . . . breathe. To relax, unwind, and slow down. Read a book. Go for a long walk. Cook your favorite meal. Pray. All of the other things will wait for you—another hour, day, week, month. Soak in the raw moments of simplicity. Don't just "get by" and "make it through another day." Find the time to decompress and bring back contentment. Relish in just being "still."

- I wish you to find comfort in the guardian angels that share your space, but soar on your own two wings and have faith conquer your fears. Release the hold you have on your dreams and let them fly across the sky. Let your mind be full of wonder.

- I wish you would know how brave you are. You are strong and mighty. You choose to work hard. You choose to take that next step. You choose to be kind. Bravery is underneath every one of those decisions.

- I wish you to live in a place of love. Do the things you love surrounded by the people you love. Do a job with dignity and pride, no matter the work, because it's important. When God opens your eyes with the morning sun, feel yourself take that cleansing breath, and settle into a moment of gratitude.

- I wish you to stop and think about the Lord designing us in His image . . . carefully and meticulously choosing every feature of our faces, every quality of our characters, every path we will take and mistakes we will make . . . and still loving us all the same.

- I wish you always find the light. Open your eyes and open your mind to shut out the darkness. The black spaces can close in on you. They can creep through the tiniest cracks and smother your flame. But the Holy Spirit is in you, working through

you. Feel the warmth and reveal the light that will
conquer the shadows.

There are days I have to search high in the hills and low in
the valleys, under rocks and stone, and scour the stars for the
good in our world. But God is everywhere, so good is everywhere. Goodness lives within the messiness. Fall in love with
that goodness surrounding you.

As the sun slips away and night falls, I want you to breathe
in the sweet scent of falling rain outside a cracked-open window. In your grandmother's kitchen, I want you to savor every
bite of her homemade apple pie that your fork digs into. As
the clouds design paintings in the sky above, I want you to
rest your weary bones and feel the warm summer breeze sail
across your skin. Through all the chaos and noise, I want you
to truly listen and hear the precious words escaping from your
children's mouths as they share their adventures of the day.

God sits with the brokenhearted. He rejoices in our happiness. He welcomes our silence, anger, frustration, tears. He
covers us with His healing hands. No matter what stage we are
at, He wants us to embrace our truth. All of it. God can turn
your hard into beautiful. He uses every ounce of our suffering for good. Bravely and boldly accept that the hurt and pain
in your life are pages in your novel. Pages that will continue
to turn. The grief and heartache will not be erased. They are
etched into the deepest parts of your soul. But . . . our Lord and
Savior—our King of Kings—our Almighty Father can build it
into miracles. The hurt is used to teach, encourage, strengthen,
and protect us.

Allowing ourselves to laugh means sadness can follow.
Allowing ourselves to love means that heartache can follow.

Nevertheless, don't hesitate to light that fire. Stoke the flames and feel the heat. There's beauty hidden amongst the ashes.

I am proof that grief and joy truly can coexist, because this is my sweet sorrow.

Made in the USA
Middletown, DE
06 December 2024

66150514R00109